THE CLINICAL SIGNIFICANCE
OF THE WORK OF BION

Donald Meltzer

THE HARRIS MELTZER TRUST

The Clinical Significance of the Work of Bion first published in 1978 by Clunie Press
for The Roland Harris Educational Trust
Combined edition of *Freud's Clinical Development, Richard Week-by-Week,*
and *The Clinical Significance of the Work of Bion* published in 1998 by Karnac Books
as *The Kleinian Development.* Reprinted in 2008 for The Harris Meltzer Trust.
New edition 2018 by The Harris Meltzer Trust
60 New Caledonian Wharf
London SE16 7TW

British Library Cataloguing in Publication Data
A C.I.P. for this book is available from the British Library

   ISBN 978 1 912567 66 9

Edited, designed and produced by The Bourne Studios
www.bournestudios.co.uk
Printed in Great Britain

www.harris-meltzer-trust.org.uk

THE CLINICAL SIGNIFICANCE
OF THE WORK OF BION

CONTENTS

ABOUT THE AUTHOR   vii

FOREWORD by Meg Harris Williams   ix

INTRODUCTION and reading list   xv

1 Experiences in groups   1

2 Re-view of 'Group dynamics' and 'The imaginary
    twin'   11

3 The schizophrenia papers   19

4 Approach to a theory of thinking   29

5 Alpha-function and beta-elements   37

6 Container and contained – the prototype of learning   47

7 The elements of psychoanalysis and psychoanalytical
    objects   55

8 The role of myth in the employment of thoughts   65

9 Psychoanalytical observation and the theory of
    transformations   75

10 Analytic truth and the operation of multiple vertices   83

11 'Learning about' as resistance to 'becoming'   91

12 The bondage of memory and desire   99

13 The psychoanalytic couple and the group   109

14 Review: catastrophic change and the mechanisms
        of defence   117

*APPENDIX: A note on Bion's concept 'reversal of
        alpha-function'*   127
INDEX   135

Donald Meltzer (1923–2004) was born in New York and studied medicine at Yale. After practising as a psychiatrist specialising in children and families, he moved to England to have analysis with Melanie Klein in the 1950s, and for some years was a training analyst with the British Society. He worked with both adults and children, and was innovative in the treatment of autistic children; in the treatment of children he worked closely with Esther Bick and Martha Harris whom he later married. He taught child psychiatry and psychoanalytic history at the Tavistock Clinic. He also took a special scholarly interest in art and aesthetics, based on a lifelong love of art. Meltzer taught widely and regularly in many countries, in Europe, Scandinavia, and North and South America, and his books have been published in many languages and continue to be increasingly influential in the teaching of psychoanalysis.

His first book, *The Psychoanalytical Process,* was published by Heinemann in 1967 and was received with some suspicion (like all his books) by the psychoanalytic establishment. Subsequent books were published by Clunie Press for the Roland Harris Educational Trust which he set up together with Martha Harris (now the Harris Meltzer Trust). The *Process* was followed by *Sexual States of Mind* in 1973, *Explorations in Autism* in 1975 (with contributions from John Bremner, Shirley Hoxter, Doreen Weddell and Isca Wittenberg); *The Kleinian Development* in 1978 (his lectures on Freud, Klein and Bion given to students at the Tavistock); *Dream Life* in 1984; *The Apprehension of Beauty* in 1988 (with Meg Harris Williams); and *The Claustrum* in 1992. *The Educational Role of the Family: A Psychoanalytical Model* (commissioned for the OECD with Martha Harris) and first published in French in 1976; a new English edition was published in 2013. As a result of his worldwide teaching several compilations exist of his supervision seminars, including *Meltzer in Barcelona* (2002), *Meltzer in Venice* (2016), *Meltzer in Sao Paulo* (2017), and *Meltzer in Paris* (2017). Other accounts by some who use his work in their own teaching practice are in *Teaching Meltzer* (2015). An introductory selection from his writings may be found in *A Meltzer Reader* (2012) and sample papers on the HMT website www.harris-meltzer-trust.org.uk.

T his book, derived like those on Freud and Klein from lectures to students, is the first serious attempt at a chronological overview of Bion's oeuvre in terms of both a philosophical quest and a model of the mind intended for use in the psychoanalytic consulting-room. Unlike many subsequent more apostolic accounts of Bion's ideas it is absorbing and even entertaining provided you have done your homework and are prepared for a roller-coaster ride through the incomprehensible (if not the 'void and formless infinite'). Meltzer is always conscious of his student audience and tackles the inevitable frustrations entailed in reading Bion by evoking a series of identifications: not only is he a student himself but so also is Bion in his attempt to discover the workings of his own mind without being deflected by its complexities. For Bion was the first to admit – not that he did not know what he was talking about – but that what he 'knew' with one part of himself he did not know with another, and in particular, could not express ('publish') since he did not have sufficient artistic equipment.

Meltzer says his account is 'not so much an exposition of Bion's ultimate thought as a record of his thinking and a document of his method of thought': nonetheless he does also build a picture of this 'thought' and the areas of the psyche which it begins to map for us. He wryly jokes how, when the 'Bion wolf' is at the door of one's intellectual house of twigs, battering at the status quo, and finally something appears to take shape and become understood, there arises a temptation to become 'a bit of a wolf oneself' in the face of other people's 'twiggy conceptions', resulting in the bad habit of 'speaking Bionese'. Instead, throughout, he tries through example to guide the reader away from projective identification and towards introjective identification – to establish through personal transparency how Bion, or some of his aspects, can link up with one's own learning from experience and illuminate its meaning in the way of his diamond-cutting analogy, sending a reciprocal shaft of light.

The lectures therefore are presented in the form of a personal investigation, conducted with quizzical self-analytic humour that is a match for Bion's own, as it were from the vertex of a younger sibling, part exasperated, part mystified and part full of admiration. 'What is this modern-day psychoanalytical Leonardo up to? What is Bion, the phenomenon, about?' What is this 'flying machine' he has created (*in Learning from Experience*) from 'bits of alpha-function' on the lines of this Kleinian baby's illusion that it can fly straight up to the breast (O) – the 'air-foil of learning theory'? OK, he only got 'off the ground' for a few scintillating seconds but then attempted another impossible ambition, in *Elements,* to astrologically map the predicted pathways of the world of thought and its three-dimensional linkages; followed by (*Transformations*) 'the navigational instruments for steering his little flying machine amongst the stars once a suitable propulsive force could be devised.' The Meltzerian metaphor is reminiscent of the childhood incident Bion relates of trying to launch a homemade aeroplane from the roof of a friend's house, which made him incoherently aware of his distance from his mother – his 'conceptual base' as Money-Kyrle would put it.

The baby-reader is understandably liable to blame the Bion-mother for his obscurities and indeed, inevitable failures. Meltzer tries to encourage the reader's negative capability, warning that our defensive reaction to the 'new idea' (whether this be embodied in Bion or in any other form) is likely to be one or all of three types: the mocker who caricatures Bion's 'beam of darkness'; the comfort-lover who knows it all anyway and puts his dozing off (just like Bion) down to 'deep contact with my patient's unconscious'; and the establishment heretic-hunter who selectively splits Bion's earlier work from its later continuation, as a means of 'loading with honours and sinking without trace'. All these pseudo-mature attitudes result in orthodoxies that are, in the Bionian sense, lies. Instead, both here and in other writings, Meltzer's procedure is to demonstrate how Bion has been 'making his way into my consulting room' and linking up with his own learning from experience.

His intellectual grasp of Bion's struggle to ensnare and formulate the wild thoughts flying about in his [psychic ambience/ penumbra of his consciousness] is formidable, and owes much to his own parallel philosophical interests; but above all to his awe regarding the nature of psychoanalytic observation. The 'power of observation, inward and outward, is the fountainhead of Bion's originality', and alpha-function (the capacity to form symbols of emotional experience) 'does not operate on the experience but on its perception' – which includes sleeping and unconscious perception, consciousness being interpreted as an 'organ for the perception of psychic qualities' (picking up a definition of Freud) which is turned outward in the day and inward at night. In order to play the 'psychoanalytic game' you must 'first make a psycho-analytical observation' – this is the crux of the matter, but Bion's view of its capturability is modified.

For at a certain point, in Meltzer's view, Bion bids a 'somewhat sad farewell to a dream of precise formulation, psychoanalytic games, rules for the practice of psychoanalysis' and surrenders himself to the uncertainties of the 'aesthetic' experience through which man can approach nearest to the truth. However the earlier flying attempts are not without fruit. They begin to find mountain-tops to land on in the later work, beginning with *Attention and Interpretation*, despite the fact that (Meltzer points out) to add to the frustration the markers provided by titles in this and other places are often not explained or even mentioned in the texts. Here Bion finally manages to 'weld together' the artistic and the scientific qualities of psychoanalysis. Throughout, Bion has been concerned 'not with evolving psychoanalytic theories but with theories about psychoanalysis as a thing-in-itself', and in a sense, redefining this very new humanistic mode of investigation on Platonic lines. Meltzer summarises the new viewpoint:

> Psychoanalysis is a method for studying the interaction of these two organizations (truth and lies) through the medium of the transference and countertransference, which can reveal the methods by which the mental pain involved in facing the truth is either modified or evaded, mainly through attacks on the linking which the growth of thought creates.
>
> But the problem of distinguishing between the evasion of pain and its modification requires reality testing, which in essence is the differentiation between truth and lies, understanding and mis-understanding. This is done by correlating the understanding derived from more than one vertex as well as by using the new thought as a pre-conception whose realization may be evaluated. (p. 98)

Unlike the splitters, Meltzer stresses the 'internal integrity of Bion's life work', evidenced in his return to the early work with groups in a way which brings this extra-Kleinian field into psychoanalytic focus as the internal group, thereby expanding the internal-family model into new realms of emotional conflict and psychopathology deriving from the nature of man as a herd animal. In the light of the mind's expanded cast of dramatis personae – functions not just family members or instincts – Bion also indicates a new range of ways in which the mind can attack itself and return to proto-mental life, including condition of 'mindlessness' (absent symbol-formation) which Meltzer takes to be one of his most important insights, one that offers the possibility of understanding such things as autism.

Bion, in his *Memoir,* lamented how rare it was to come by 'austere criticism' as distinct from 'complacent hostility' or its counterpart 'fantastic admiration'. In presenting this pioneering work of austere criticism, Meltzer did not expect either students or colleagues to 'agree' with his reading; he did perhaps hope that they might follow his example that is geared at introjectively identifying, that is, incorporating Bion into one of a personal pantheon of internal teaching objects. He has not, he admits, taken to playing psychoanalytic games with the Grid in the evenings instead of watching television; but nonetheless Bion's mode of exploration has filtered into his psychoanalytic practice and the 'new idea' has changed it for ever. Perhaps the most effective way to maintain an attitude of learning-from-Bion is to remember that he considered thinking to be (as Martha Harris expresses it) 'a human activity still in its absolute infancy'. Bion is not an authority, he is a guide to learning to think for oneself, albeit this appeared to him 'something of a race against time'.

Meg Harris Williams
(editor)

Although this book can be read on its own, clearly its intention was to link the work of Bion, particularly in its clinical application, to the line of development in psychoanalysis leading from Freud through Abraham to Melanie Klein and on to Wilfred Bion. In the two earlier volumes a selective attention was given first to the clinical writings of Freud, with emphasis on the evolution of his methods of observation, the clinical data thrown up and finally the formulations that were reached, treating them not so much as scientific theories as metaphoric devices for organizing description of phenomena. Next the *Narrative* was examined in detail, week by week, as the clinical reference point for describing the evolution of Melanie Klein's formulations of mental development and psychopathology, highlighting along the way the evidences of her clinical methods of observation, thought and communication. The first two volumes therefore followed different methods of exposition: the first chronological, the second focussed, looking both backward and forward on the history of Mrs Klein's thought. In the present volume the chronological method is taken up again, with respect to the date of the clinical work if not always the date of publication. Thus, for instance, the papers republished in *Second Thoughts* will be dealt with earlier than the second thoughts themselves. The emphasis of the book will be on Bion's methods of observation and thought, again, as with Freud and Melanie Klein, rather neglecting the theories as an explanatory system. This should not be taken as value judgment, dismissive of the theoretical aspects, but rather as a manifestation of the method of exposition being followed and the underlying purpose. The intention in these three volumes has been to trace the continuity of clinical method and thought from Freud to Bion in order to establish on firm ground the conception of the 'Kleinian Development'. This view is not tenable in the realm of theory, where a very marked discontinuity is clearly in evidence, both from Freud to Klein and from Klein to Bion. Freud has constructed a quasi-neurophysiological explanatory system which never departed in its foundations from the preconceptions of the *Project for a Scientific Psychology*. Melanie Klein constructed a quasi-theological system in which internal objects have the significance of deity. Bion has constructed a quasi-philosophical system where thought sits amazed in Plato's cave straining itself to apprehend the noumena of the world. Each of these systems, *qua* system, has its area of interest and appeal but scant clinical application. In studying the work of Bion, then, the stress will be laid, to borrow his words, on those elements which are 'meant for use in the consulting room'.

The present volume was presented as lectures to the fourth-year students of the Tavistock Child Psychotherapy Course, along with other members of the clinic staff and guests, in 1976–77 and 1977–78. They were constructed on the assumption that the audience would have read the relevant work of Bion in the week prior to presentation and thus have the text clearly in mind. For this reason the book cannot be very profitably read by anyone who does not follow the same discipline. In contrast to the lectures on Freud and Klein, which were delivered extemporaneously, with the exception of rare direct quotations, the present lectures on Bion, because of the intricacy of the argument and the frequent need for quotation, were read out and followed by a period of discussion.

Reading list of works by Bion

(1948). *Experiences in Groups*. Reprinted: London: Tavistock, 1961.

(1950). The imaginary twin. In *Second Thoughts* (1967).

(1952). Group dynamics: a review. *International Journal of Psychoanalysis*, 33: 235–247. Reprinted in *Experiences in Groups* (1961).

(1953). Notes on the theory of schizophrenia. In *Second Thoughts* (1967).

(1956). Development of schizophrenic thought. *International Journal of Psychoanalysis*, 37: 334–346. Reprinted in *Second Thoughts* (1967).

(1957). On arrogance. Read to the Psychoanalytic Congress, Paris. In *Second Thoughts* (1967).

(1957). Differentiation of the psychotic from the non-psychotic personalities. *International Journal of Psychoanalysis*, 38: 266–275. Reprinted in *Second Thoughts* (1967).

(1958). On hallucination. *International Journal of Psychoanalysis*, 39: 341–349. Reprinted in *Second Thoughts* (1967).

(1959). Attacks on linking. *International Journal of Psychoanalysis*, 40: 308–315. Reprinted in *Second Thoughts* (1967).

(1962). A theory of thinking. *International Journal of Psychoanalysis*, 43: 306–310. Reprinted in *Second Thoughts* (1967).

(1962). *Learning from Experience*. London: Tavistock.

(1963). *Elements of Psychoanalysis*. London: Heinemann.

(1965). *Transformations*. London: Heinemann.

(1966). Catastrophic change. Bulletin of the British Psychoanalytical Society no. 5.

(1967). *Second Thoughts*. London: Maresfield.

(1970). *Attention and Interpretation*. London: Tavistock.

(1975–1979). *A Memoir of the Future*. 3 vols: *The Dream* (Brazil: Imago); *The Past Presented* (Brazil: Imago); *The Dawn of Oblivion* (Perthshire: Clunie Press).

CHAPTER ONE

Experiences in Groups

xperiences in Groups is the work of three different periods in Bion's life: military psychiatric, in wartime, age 40 (pre-view), civilian psychiatric in peacetime (experiences) age 50, and psychoanalytic (re-view), age 60. Never task- or result oriented, the key word is always 'experience', later to be formalized as the basis of 'learning from experience' as against 'learning about' things, and finally formulated as 'transformations in O' and 'becoming O'. The military psychiatrist who had to form a training wing for the rehabilitation of neurotic soldiers saw his task as one of restoring these men to integration in a disciplined community from a state of subjugation to the 'helplessness' of neurosis. His thesis was that the restoration of discipline as an internal fact required participation in an external discipline, which in its turn depended on two factors: (1) the presence of the enemy and (2) 'the presence of an officer who, being experienced, knows some of his own failings, respects the integrity of his men, and is not afraid of either their good will or their hostility.'

It is of interest to note Bion's emphasis on the qualities of the person in responsibility, for at no point in this little paper does he minimize for the sake of the appearance of modesty the impact of his personality on this group of 300–400 men. And he seems able to do this without immodesty by virtue of this assumption: 'being experienced, etc'. While at no point does he enlarge on this extraordinary assumption that 'experience' produces these valuable qualities of self-knowledge, respect for others and fearlessness in the face of others' emotions, one can only suppose that he already had in his mind a quite idiosyncratic usage for the word.

But what of this 'presence of the enemy'? It is characteristic of Bion's playfulness that he should use ambiguity to allow the reader both to misconstrue his meaning and to remain puzzled and uncertain for some time before clarification arrives. It is evident that these men are in a hospital and not in the 'presence of the enemy'. We have to wait for the bottom of the page to find out that the enemy is 'neurosis as a disability of the community'. Reading Bion is perhaps not very different from being in one of his groups, where his fearlessness takes the form of a playful patience in the interest of allowing others to have experiences. The reader is so exposed to these experiences that he has not the slightest difficulty in believing in the impatience and exasperation of the members of the groups when faced with this immovable body.

These two contrasting usages of language, ambiguity and idiosyncracy, are essential tools of Bion's methods of both investigation and exposition. The search for ambiguity will lead him to more and more mathematical formulations as the years go by, while his idiosyncratic use of language will achieve a poetic syntax quite distinctive; so distinctive in fact that his impact on other peoples' modes and content of thought can be traced, like a radioactive compound, circulating in the stream of their language usage.

When we turn to the ten-years' older Bion of the therapeutic groups we find virtually the same elements at work as those employed to institute discipline among the soldiers of the training wing. His humour is not just a matter of literary style, even if literary style is used to amplify it. 'It was disconcerting to find that the Committee seemed to believe that patients could be cured in such groups as these ... Indeed the only cure of which

I could speak with certainty was related to a minor symptom of my own – a belief that groups might take kindly to my efforts.' It is a humour that emanates from a very particular position as observer-participant, compounded of the qualities that he had enumerated for the 'experienced' officer plus an ability to see the situation from many different angles. This will later be formulated as the concept of 'vertices', the necessity for 'binocular vision', and the phenomenon of 'reversible perspective'. But in this early work it manifests itself in two particular ways. For instance:

> Most members (of the group) had been told that I would 'take' the group; some say that I have a reputation for knowing a lot about groups; some feel that I ought to explain what we are going to do; some thought it was going to be a kind of seminar, or perhaps a lecture. When I draw attention to the fact that these ideas seem to me to be hearsay, there seems to be a feeling that I am attempting to deny my eminence as a 'taker' of groups'.

Or: 'It would be very useful if we could feel that when we have made observations of this kind they corresponded to facts.' This first manifestation, the differentiation between hearsay and observation of facts, runs through Bion's work and will result in an emphasis on the role of the 'selected fact' for creative thought.

The second manifestation of his capacity to see things from different angles, and with consequent humour, is his alertness to paradox and 'surprising contradiction'. The qualities of mind which make for this alertness are not in evidence in this early work but will be investigated by Bion later in his preoccupation with the psychoanalytical method, resulting in the emphasis on the moment of experience needing to be guarded from 'memory' and 'desire' in order to be apprehended in its uniqueness. This has an important link with his attitude towards language: that it can be either a powerful and irreplaceable instrument of thought, or its greatest deterrent: 'We have to recognize that perhaps the members of the group assume too easily that the label on the box is a good description of the contents.' But the humour is not the only emanation coming from this ability to see things from many different angles. It is probably also the basis of the modesty of presentation which can easily strike the reader as affected in a man of such eminence. 'The articles printed here aroused more interest than I expected', or 'The fact that the interpretations would seem to be concerned with matters of no importance to anyone but myself' could appear facetious if one did not comprehend Bion's awe of the complexity of the phenomena he sets out to investigate and describe. He is clearly sincere when he indicates that his intention is 'to provide as much material as possible for the reader to use in reaching his own conclusions'. It is not clear whether Bion in fact considers that the complexity inheres in the phenomena themselves or whether it is a function of the complexity of the mind that studies them, that it can only see them in the round and in full emotional colour when it employs its imagination from different points of view simultaneously. In any event his modesty is deeply rooted in respect for both phenomena of the mind and the difficulty of gaining and transmitting knowledge of them: 'phenomena whose existence I have only been able to indicate by descriptions of facts that bear less relationship to the object of our study than the lines of a monochrome print do to the colours of a painting in which colour is the all-important quality'.

We will have many opportunities in the course of our study of Bion's work to amplify this initial appraisal of the particular qualities of mind and character which he has brought to bear on the phenomena of the analytical consulting room, but it seems of special interest to gain some view of the pre-analytical Bion and of the equipment he brought into the field, to distinguish it from the techniques and modes of thought he developed from the special experience of psychoanalysis. So we may now turn our attention to modes of thought that are exhibited in *Experiences*, recognizing that these cannot sharply be distinguished from character and qualities of mind.

Early in the *Experiences* we meet a mode of thought which Bion, on the model of the use of a microscope, calls 'altered focus'. This is not to be confused with binocular vision, which seems to refer particularly to the points of view natural to the different mentalities involved in any situation. Altered focus would seem to imply that the instrument of observation, comparable to the microscope playing upon a thick section, is a variable model of the structure of the situation being observed. The example he gives involves two different models: in one there is a group of people meeting and interacting, from which group two members are absent; in the second model there is a group of people interacting, some of whom are present and two of whom are absent. These two foci seem to be able to throw light on one another if they are seen also to reveal systems of thought, feeling and behaviour that interact. This is a mode of thought because it is a device that can be used for enhancing observation and reflection, while the binocular vision is an expression of character in that it is the natural mode of experience of an individual who, by contact with different parts of his personality, is able to identify with different roles in human interaction and perception.

Another characteristic mode of thought for Bion is the framing of hypotheses as instruments of observation, to be tested for their utility in widening the field of scrutiny and thereby its phenomenological comprehensibility. This differs significantly from the use of the hypothesis in Baconian science as a frame work for the construction of experiment and of eliciting proof or refutation:

> I shall postulate a group mentality as a pool to which the anonymous contributions are made and through which the impulses and desires implicit in these contributions are gratified ... I shall expect the group mentality to be distinguished by a uniformity that contrasted with the diversity of thought in the mentality of the individuals ... If experience shows that this hypothesis fulfils a useful function, further characteristics of the group mentality may be added from clinical observation.

In other words the utility of the hypothesis will not only be manifest by clarification of the phenomena it is meant to assist in observing, but will also lead to observations which will make possible the expansion and clarification of the hypothesis.

Very striking is Bion's use of negative evidence and his trust in it as a guideline to the formation of hypotheses. For instance: 'I shall assume nevertheless that unless a group actively disavows its leader it is, in fact, following him ... I dare say that it will be possible to base belief in the complicity of the group on something more convincing than negative evidence, but for the time being I regard negative evidence as good enough.' This is more reminiscent of Jesus than Pasteur, but this is not surprising when one remembers Bion's later repudiation of the medical model for psychoanalysis. The point about negative evidence in the field of psychological research would seem to rest upon the thesis that a function of which the mental apparatus is capable cannot be simply absent or suspended, as can physiological, including neurophysiological, functions; only manipulation of its relationship to other functions, including the function of consciousness, can be effected, simulating absence.

Having briefly investigated Bion's qualities of mind as they are revealed in this book and then some of his characteristic modes of thought, it might be useful to turn to the type of experience to which his reader is exposed, for the stressfulness of reading his work is not to be minimized. It is easy, under this stress, to assume that his modes of thought are difficult or that his methods of exposition are obscure. But I think that neither of these is particularly true, and furthermore that, even if they are to some degree, they are not the source of the stress. It is to be found in identification processes, that is identification with members of the groups he is treating (and in later papers with his patients in analysis) and in failure of identification with Bion himself. Let us examine these two in turn, for recognition of their role may both lessen the painfulness of the reading and thereby increase the ease of comprehension.

Identification with the members of the group is conducive to exasperation for a simple reason: that Bion's primary thesis in work with groups is that he is 'not concerned to give individual treatment in public, but to draw attention to the actual experiences of the group'. While this may have been difficult for the members to bear, it is doubly difficult for the reader who is alone with the book and not in a group atmosphere. The frustration becomes seasoned with humiliation when told that 'the exasperation, at first sight so reasonable, of the patient whose pressing personal difficulty is being ignored, is dictated, not so much by the frustration of a legitimate aim, as by the exposure of difficulties the patient had not come to discuss, and in particular his characteristics as a group member.'

On the other hand identification with Bion as leader is constantly blocked by feelings of inferiority. For instance: 'If the psychiatrist can manage boldly to use the group instead of spending his time more or less unconsciously apologizing for his presence' or, 'it may be helpful for the psychiatrist who has a taste for trying my methods in a group to remember that few things in history have aroused a group's feelings more powerfully than controversy about the characteristics of the deity whose cult is at the time flourishing' (referring to investigation of the psychiatrist as leader and deity of the dependent basic assumption group). The certainty of not having the requisite 'boldness' and there-fore of having no 'taste for trying [Dr Bion's] methods' crowds in upon the reader in a daunting way.

Perhaps the next useful step in our investigation of this early work of Bion, since our aim is to outline the special equipment he brought with him to psychoanalysis, might be to trace some of what might be called his postulates, for he does sometimes call them this himself. They are perhaps, in relation to the research being described, in the nature of preconceptions rather than real-izations growing out of the experiences in groups. They throw a useful light on his approach to problems of the mind.

Perhaps the most important one is the idea of a 'proto-mental' level of function, an idea which appears in this book but not, to my recollection, anywhere explicitly in his later work. As always in reading Bion it is important to remember that, in proposing this postulate for understanding the way in which the emotions connected with the basic assumptions are bound inextricably to one another, he is not suggesting a theory or solution but only proposing a model because it might prove 'convenient' and 'useful', and furthermore that there is 'no harm' in so doing, provided it is not taken to describe a cause and effect series. The idea is that there is a proto-mental level at which physical and psychological events are not differentiated, where the emotional components are fused because incipient as observable psycho-logical phenomena. This has a strong link to Freud's concept of primary narcissism as a level at which object relation and iden-tification are undifferentiated and where the ego is still purely a body-ego. But it is also different, for Bion is approaching groups on the assumption that man is a herd animal and that his most primitive mentality is overwhelmingly concerned with his membership of groups. From that point of view individual relationships would derive their meaning from their origin in pairing groups.

This leads on to a second postulate, namely that the group phenomena he is studying are radically different from those of the family. This is fundamentally different from Freud's approach in *Group Psychology* where he assumed that the family was the basic model and that the roles of individuals could be extrapolated for groups from those observed in family life. The liberating effect of Bion's postulate is the best evidence that it was a postulate indeed, rather than a realization, for it first of all clearly liberated Bion from having to play any of the roles that the group wished to impose upon him, whether under basic assumption or in the work group. This perhaps needs to be grasped in order for the reader to be freed from identification with the group members in their exasperation, and to grasp the magnitude of achievement it made possible. Of course having such a postulate may have armed Bion against the acceptance of roles imposed by the group but it is clear that long struggle was required to learn to implement it. The consequence was a field of study for group phenomena in every way comparable to the field of the transference in psychoanalysis, where the participant-observer could employ the binocular vision of simultaneous inward and outward scrutiny.

Taken together these two postulates imply that man's primitive heritage makes it necessary for him to be a member of a group and that he has mental equipment for doing this of two different sorts, making possible his participation in two contrasting groupings: the basic assumption group (Ba) and the work group (W) (at first called the 'sophisticated group'). Involvements in the Ba group are managed at the proto-mental level, where emotional reactions are undifferentiated from physical ones and where impulses express themselves in directional tendencies (he calls it 'valency' and likens it to tropism) rather than in phantasy or planning. The capacity of Ba states for instantaneous spread in the group is matched by their deeply unconscious position, making them far more easily evident to an observer than to the subjects themselves. In contrast, participation in the W group is managed by phantasy with easy access to consciousness; it is bound to reality and therefore to development through learning from experience. Despite its handicaps of cumbersome procedure and disunity in comparison with, and in conflict with, the tendency to basic assumption organization, 'it is the W group that triumphs in the long run'. A comforting message, despite lack of specificity as to the duration of this 'long run'!

In this scheme it would seem that individuality arises from experience of the work group, paleontologically speaking; that is, out of the emergence of the family from the matrix of the tribe. This is an important implication of Bion's point of view, but must be taken as part of the system of postulates that makes up the point of view or vertex from which he is approaching mental phenomena. He then uses it as one focus to juxtapose to the focus adopted, say, by Freud, in order to frame the hypotheses be wishes to use, and to test for usefulness, not for correctness. It should be kept in mind that Bion's conception of human science is phenomenological and, as will be clear in his later work, mystical. The widening of consciousness, and thus of observation and thought, is his aim, not proof and explanation. The hypotheses which grow out of this postulate ground revolve about the nature of conflict in groups, that is between Ba and W as well as among the three different Ba groups – dependent (D), pairing (P) and fight-flight (F). The description of the uses of this hypothesis and the phenomena they reveal forms the body of *Experiences in Groups* and need not be summarized here. What is needed instead, with a view to our study of Bion's later work, is to trace further the implications of this structure of hypothesis for a vertex on the individual mentality as it is studied in psychoanalysis. One implication is that the psychoanalytical method consists of two operations, one being the formation of a two-member W group for studying the phenomena of the other the BaP (basic assumption pairing) of the transference. This BaP has its origins in the child's experience of the family in the light of the Oedipus conflict, in which the pairing couple (primal scene and combined object) is the centre of interest. It stands in contrast with the child's experience of the family as W, a work-group of two parents met for the purpose of raising children, for instance.

A second implication would be that the study of the transference would involve noting the fluctuations from Oedipus conflict (BaP) to other Ba groupings – BaD (infantile dependence, splitting and idealization, narcissistic self-idealization, etc.) and BaF (paranoid-schizoid position, delinquent narcissistic organization, delusion formation, etc.). This point of view could enrich the analyst's study of acting out and of the interaction between the analysis and other areas of the patient's (and analyst's) life. The notion that these Ba functions can simmer on at a proto-mental level could add a new dimension to the analyst's scrutiny of dreams, one quite different from elucidation of unconscious (latent) meaning. It would add a new dimension to the concept of conflict. Where would one place it? Inter- or intra-systemic, for instance.

In closing this first chapter it is necessary to emphasize the chronology of our study. It will have been evident that thus far only the pre-view and the seven papers on 'experiences' have been discussed, as the aim was to draw a baseline of the preanalytic Bion. It is true that he was already studying psychoanalysis at the time of the actual work of 'taking' the groups, but the conceptual framework and language are not strictly psychoanalytical. The 're-view', written several years later, will be left for consideration along with one of the early psychoanalytical papers republished in *Second Thoughts*. In drawing this base-line, attention has been paid to a number of aspects: the qualities of mind and character, modes of thought, language usage, scientific method (and by implication, philosophy of science), literary style and its impact on the reader, structure of postulates and use of hypotheses. Very little attention has been paid to the actual theory of groups or therapeutic method with groups, as that will have been evident to the reader and is somewhat aside from the purpose of this book.

CHAPTER TWO

Re-view of 'Group dynamics' and 'The imaginary twin'

I n the first chapter an attempt was made to draw out the prepsychoanalytic Bion by the use of the first two sections of *Experiences in Groups*, the clinical work for which probably extended from 1942 through 1950. Some evaluation of the special equipment he brought into the field of psychoanalysis was attempted, bearing on his character, his modes of thought, the background of his special humour, his philosophy of science, his use of language and his basic differentiation between individual and group mentality.

In the present chapter we are concerned to examine Bion's transition into the field of psychoanalysis, which occurred through his association with John Rickman and his training analysis with Melanie Klein. The review of his work on groups in the light of the work of Freud and Melanie Klein should show us something of the impact of psychoanalytical experience and thought on his previous ideas and attitudes. His first clinical paper in analysis, 'The imaginary twin', might be expected to show him working in the consulting room so that we can compare the man in these two therapeutic settings, group and individual. It is perhaps worthwhile to remember the historical setting of his work. For instance, Melanie Klein's great paper on projective identification and splitting processes ('Notes on some schizoid mechanisms') had appeared in 1946 while the 1950s were characterized by the opening up of the phenomenon of the countertransference for clinical use by such figures as Winnicott, Paula Heimann, and Money-Kyrle. The severe disputes in the British Society over issues of theory and technique raised by Mrs Klein's work had settled down to a 'gentlemen's agreement' which held the society together and created a fairly electric atmosphere for research and discussion. Bion became director of the clinic a few years after qualification and stirred great interest by his papers on psychosis.

The first problem *vis à vis* the psychoanalytical community raised by his work with groups was that of the highly subjective nature of the observations:

> It can be justly argued that interpretations for which the strongest evidence lies, not in the observed facts in the group but in the subjective reactions of the analyst, are more likely to find their explanation in the psycho-pathology of the analyst than in the dynamics of the group. It is a just criticism, and one which will have to be met by years of careful work by more than one analyst, but for that very reason I shall leave it on one side ... (p. 148)

But Bion is not content to forestall criticism, for he has a very positive and original contribution to make to the study of countertransference and its relation to projective identification which is hidden here and not taken up elsewhere in the literature until the work of Racker in the 1960s, and Grinberg in the 1970s with his concept of projective counter-identification. Bion writes:

> Now the experience of counter-transference appears to me to have quite a distinct quality that should enable the analyst to differentiate the occasion when he is the object of a projective identification from the occasion when he is not. The analyst feels he is being manipulated so as to be playing a part, no matter how difficult to recognize, in somebody else's phantasy – or he would do if it were not for what in recollection I can only call a temporary loss of insight, a sense of experiencing strong feelings and at the same time a belief

that their existence is quite adequately justified by the objective situation . . . (p. 149)

These criteria for identifying an experience of being the object of a projective identification: namely a temporary loss of insight during an emotional experience whose quality seems un questionably justified, followed by insight and the feeling of having been dominated by someone else's phantasy, make a satisfactory scientific instrument of what promised to be a technique for wholesale self-justification by analysts. The key is the experience of having been manipulated to play a role in someone else's phantasy, the realization of which is accompanied by anxiety and humiliation leading to retaliatory impulse.

By means of this conception Bion makes the link between his work with groups and with individuals quite compelling and gives substance to the hope of bringing a binocular vision to bear on mental functions. The basic technique of psychoanalysis of examining the transference from a position which is both inside and outside the relationship is made applicable to groups through this recognition of the possibility of losing and recovering insight. But it is not quite clear what position Bion adopts regarding the essential relationship of group mentality to individual mentality. In the earlier papers where the postulate of a proto-mental system was put forward as a tool for examining the observations it seemed likely that the two systems were quite separate but with a linkage. This linkage seemed to be forged in the unconscious at a juncture of narcissistic organization (though Bion does not directly suggest this) and the basic assumptions that are in abeyance at the moment and held at the proto-mental level. In this psychoanalytical re-view he brings the two together by way of the Oedipus conflict and the concepts of primitive splitting and identification processes at a part-object level: 'On the emotional plane, where basic assumptions are dominant, Oedipal figures... can be discerned in the material just as they are in a psychoanalysis. But they include one component of the Oedipus myth of which little has been said, and that is the sphinx' (p. 162).

Here is an instance where one suspects that the special qualities, sphinx-like, of Bion have obtruded themselves on the material, but he insists that this is inevitable where the group includes anyone with a 'questioning attitude'. The fears thrown up by this attitude 'approximate ... to very primitive phantasies about the contents of the mother's body' and sets in motion defences 'characteristic of the paranoid-schizoid position'. The pairing group is consequently seen as bound closely to the primal scene at a primitive level, the dependent group to the breast relationship as partial object, the fight-flight group to paranoid anxieties connected with splitting-and-idealization. Consequently a continuous spectrum of degree of disturbance now is seen to link the basic assumption group to the work group and 'the more stable the group, the more it corresponds to Freud's description of the group as a repetition of family group patterns and neurotic mechanisms'. This has the appearance of a climbdown from a more radical position. The emotional colouring of the basic assumption group is no longer a manifestation of valency but can be described with the words used for individual emotions, for 'there is much to suggest that these supposed "basic assumptions" cannot be regarded as distinct states of mind'; by which he means distinct from one another but also from the individual mentality, probably. Again the equivocation sounds rather like a climbdown in the face of the intimidating impact of the psychoanalytical basic assumption group.

If viewed in this way the brilliance of Bion's rapprochement to Freud's views is quite disturbing. His assimilation of the church, army and aristocracy to the dependent, fight-flight and pairing groups respectively leaves open the possibility of considering psychoanalysis, for example, a special instance of the pairing group and thus naturally preoccupied with sex. In this way group and individual mentality are brought absolutely together as merely 'special instances' of one another: 'The apparent difference between group psychology and individual psychology is an illusion produced by the fact that the group brings into prominence phenomena that appear alien to an observer unaccustomed to using the group' (p. 169). That sounds a very sophisticated apologia and recantation. The impression is reinforced when Bion asserts, 'I have been forced to the conclusion that verbal exchange is a function of the work group' and that the basic assumption group communicated its valencies and generates its unanimity by 'debased' rather than 'primitive' methods – that is, its efforts lack symbol formation and are more in the nature of actions than communications. And here he brings in the myth of the Tower of Babel, which he will come back to twenty years on.

Bearing in mind the suggestion that the impact of psychoanalytical training upon the community concerned with this had an intimidating effect temporarily, we must turn to Bion's first clinical paper. From the outset the Bionic atmosphere is in evidence in the terse description of selected facts and pithy observations, with a clear evidence of patiently waiting for phenomena to make their impact upon the analyst. And when they do, the binocular vision is immediately evidenced, 'as if two quite separate scansions of his material were possible'. Also Bion's feeling for language is searching out the ambiguities, paradoxes and equivocations with an acuteness very reminiscent of Freud. But listen to him speak to the patient who has just suggested that the analysis is fruitless: 'I replied that although estimations of progress in analysis were difficult to make there was no reason why we should not accept his evaluation as correct.' He goes on to examine the meaning of 'treatment' and its implications, one of which being 'that the alleviation of symptoms was sometimes achieved by factors incidental to analysis; for example the sense of security obtained from feeling there was someone to go to'. The impressive aspect is the representation of the 'questioning attitude' which does not shy from serious consideration of unpleasant possibilities threatening the very foundation of the undertaking. But note also that Bion is willing to consider that the 'security obtained from feeling there was someone to go to' was 'incidental to analysis'.

This is worth noting because it is linked to the report of an incident in the analysis which shows that his view of the procedure was very closely bound to the concept of the 'mutative interpretation' (Strachey) and Mrs Klein's trust in 'correct' interpretation. The way in which Bion has construed the patient's association about the complaining woman (S.T., p.7), which followed the silence attendant to his statement about factors 'incidental', is impressive as a possibility. But he may also have felt himself 'packed off ' by Bion and experienced the rhythm of 'association–interpretation–association' as interpretation–association–interpretation: that is, being held under Bion's control and packed off with soporific interpretations of a so-called tramline sort, as suggested by statements such as: 'There was plenty of Oedipal material, produced on a most superficial level, which I duly interpreted.' Duly and dully.

This suggests that Bion was experiencing a sort of psychoanalytical latency period in which dutifulness was indeed dulling his creativity – and perhaps his critical judgment. It strikes one as strange to hear him make such vague catechistic statements as, 'When I had recovered from my surprise, I remembered that we had often had reason to suppose that he felt he had a poisonous family inside him but that was the first occasion on which I had had such a dramatic exhibition of himself in the act of introjecting objects.' It is puzzling to find no 'second thoughts' about this section (14) in the commentary of twenty years later.

The dream which followed the session in which the 'twin' was first interpreted confirms that Bion was felt to have blocked the patient's egress from analysis in a cleverly spiteful way but does not cover the earlier operation in which the patient in his car 'kept abreast' of the other car, 'conforming to its movements', which might suggest, for instance, that, when the breastfeed stopped, the nipple became split off and turned into a persecutor, perhaps indistinguishable from a bad part of the self. The point is not to plead that this would improve Bion's interpretation but to remove the dazzle from his work, induced by his use of language, so as to notice the drop in his creativity of thought that this paper represents. It is a paper devoted to the already familiar subject of split-off bad parts and is a confirmation of Mrs Klein's findings dressed up in Bion's unique style.

Similarly in the 'curled up or rigid' material (p. 10), Bion displays a typical indifference to the critical aspects of the patient's material (for instance that the big bill of the dream might refer to his making such long and prolix interpretations), typical that is of psychoanalytical papers and so uncharacteristic of Bion himself. But in the midst of this disappointing paper in which a preconceived theoretical framework is imposed on rather recalcitrant material, that is, the central theme of the imaginary twin, sparkling bits of material appear giving evidence of Bion's restiveness under the restraint of psychoanalytical theory (much like his patient's feeling about being curled up and in danger of the cramp).

It seems fairly clear from most of the paper that Bion had been learning to practice analysis properly – listening, observing, interpreting. But it is also clear that his interpretations in analysis now, unlike his work with the groups, were explanatory rather than descriptive. 'The fear of his aggression, closely linked in his mind with faeces, caused him to retreat to a position in which he felt constrained and confined and thus secure from …' etc. It is only quietly, as if on tiptoe, that the uniqueness of his approach begins to assert itself. It can be seen in an operation that is characteristic of his work but will not be made explicit for another twenty years. This is his capacity to observe the transactions in the consulting room as if they were all a dream and to listen to a patient's account of his life in the outside world as if it were the account of a dream.

The material that demonstrates this relates to what he calls 'the manner in which the patient was able to bring his material into consciousness'. Bion clearly treats the patient's reports 'in terms of play therapy with a child', that is, as phantasy or dream-equivalent. The result is a fascinating account of the patient's attempts at reality testing by means of unisensual scrutiny, first with the eyes, then the nose, the ears, the mouth, etc., over which series the intellect is then to preside and judge. At this point Bion is inclined to consider this a tenable method, but later in his work (*Learning from Experience*, 1963) he will recognize the fallibility of the serial testing in comparison with what he will puckishly call 'common sense'.

Finally, a point about the 'two speculations' (p. 20), which grow out of this thesis of the imaginary twin. The first has to do with the connection between the personification of splits in the personality and symbol formation, suggesting a 'capacity' that is variable from person to person and from time to time. Both of these items, the personification, and the role of symbol formation, are very closely bound to Mrs Klein's work, and are not the most creative aspects of it. This is, or can easily be taken for, apostolic behaviour.

The second speculation about the role of vision in the material of the three patients terminates weakly: 'For myself, I have found it impossible to interpret the material presented to me by these patients as a manifestation of purely psychological development divorced from any concurrent physical development. I have wondered whether the psychological development was bound up with the development of ocular control in the same way that problems of development linked with oral aggression co-exist with the eruption of teeth'. What a far cry from the boldness with which he could postulate a proto-mental system!

In summary then, a fairly unmistakeable impression results from taking these two papers, the 'Re-view' and 'Imaginary twin', together; namely, that psychoanalytical training has had an oppressive effect upon Bion. It is perhaps one of the great limitations of this sort of training that the personal analysis takes so long to 'recover from', to use a phrase Bion employed in 1976 in his lecture at the Tavistock Centre. In this regard one should note that all Bion's major publications came after the death of Mrs Klein in 1960.

CHAPTER THREE

The schizophrenia papers

I t is perhaps difficult for people unacquainted with the use of the concepts of splitting and projective identification, as well as for those who have become perhaps a little blasé about them, to realize the electrifying impact of Mrs Klein's 1946 paper, 'Notes on some schizoid mechanisms', upon the analysts who were working closely with her. With the notable exception of Bion's later work it could be said that the history of the next thirty years of research could be written in terms of the phenomenology and implications of these two seminal concepts.

Thus in approaching the papers written by Bion in the years 1953 to 1958 one immediately is struck by this aspect of the content in its application to the phenomena of the psychotic, and especially the schizophrenic patient. The 1950s were in a sense the heyday of psychoanalytical interest in the psychoses and the literature swells with contributions to their metapsychology and reports of successful treatment by psychological methods. In the latter category, especially the work done in America at that time by people like Frieda Fromm Reichmann, John Rosen, Milton Wexler; or in France by Mme Sechehaye, turned largely upon the modification of the psychoanalytical method to the treatment of these disorders. While this was intended to be an adaptation in the technical sense, by which means the analytical method had been made suitable to the treatment of children by Mrs Klein and Miss Freud, for instance, a great deal of methodological confusion reigned. It was not perhaps realized that, at least as far as Melanie Klein's adaptation of the method was concerned, the intention had been to alter nothing in the method, but to facilitate the means of communication available to the patient. This was not so true of Miss Freud's early work, largely on the basis of an assumption that the child would not be able to form a transference in the same sense as the adult patient. That assumption was based in turn upon a view of the transference that stressed its 'transfer' from the past under the sway of the repetition compulsion rather than viewing it as an externalization of internal object relations under the pressure of the immediate operation of impulse and anxiety.

The confusion of method that resulted from the gross modifications of the setting: in the behaviour of the analyst, the substitution of action for verbal interpretation (non-verbal interpretation), rendered results incomparable and generated a fragmentation of the psychoanalytical community which was trying to adapt the method for use in mental hospitals as well as to widen the scope for out-patient treatment. Added to this was another dimension of confusion based upon the use of a nosology borrowed from descriptive psychiatry which was far too gross to differentiate categories of illness relevant to a method based on metapsychology. Accordingly the term schizophrenia, for instance, was so variously used in clinical reports that evaluation of the utility of technical modifications became virtually impossible.

Bion, along with other people such as Rosenfeld and Segal who were working with psychotics at that time, chose to follow the technical tradition of Mrs Klein in adapting the method by altering nothing but the means of communication available to the patient, and this they did in fact by widening the scope of their powers of observation. Naturally this took the form of paying greater attention, as in child analysis, to the actions of the patient in the consulting room. But it also extended to a new area of phenomenology, the uses of language. Here psychoanalysts such as Bion, who had had a classical as well as medical education, were in a position to profit from the great developments in semantics, linguistics, communication theory and mathematics that had commenced in the 1920s (Russell and Whitehead, the Vienna Circle, the later Wittgenstein). This in turn focussed attention on problems of symbol formation, notational systems, modes of thought, uses of ambiguity, the meaning of silences, the role of the musical versus the lexical level in communication, etc.

In this historical context, inside and outside psychoanalysis, the papers of the 1953–58 period (a meagre production and in many ways repetitive) are significant in two directions which may be most profitably and lucidly discussed separately; the direction of research into the schizoid mechanisms and the phenomenology of the paranoid-schizoid and depressive positions in the psychoses, and, secondly, the application to the psychoanalytical method of concepts borrowed from philosophy, mathematics and linguistics, enhancing both the scope of observation and the complexity of thought applied to them, both in and outside the consulting room. Bion the apostle and Bion the messiah, taking these terms as applicable to daily life in no exotic sense.

One must also, therefore, in discussing the apostolic aspect of these papers, remember where the development of Mrs Klein's thought had reached at this time. The description of schizoid mechanisms came as an investigation of the details of the paranoid-schizoid position at a time when she was still considering these two positions as the fixation points respectively for schizophrenia and manic-depressive psychosis. They occurred in the baby's development in the first year of life characteristically and meant that the infant suffered from states of mind that were in all their essentials equivalent to the adult psychoses, taken as regressive states in Freud's sense. Although she denied that this was tantamount to saying that babies are psychotic, it is difficult to see how this implication could be escaped. Only gradually did this view of paranoid-schizoid and depressive position as developmental phases give way to their application as economic principles, finally tersely summarized by Bion himself as $Ps \leftrightarrow D$.

Therefore the view or model of schizophrenia that Bion is using in these papers in not really consonant with Freud's construction in the Schreber case, of a quiet 'world-destruction' phase of the disease followed by the noisy 'recovery' phase of delusional system formation in which the 'world' (not quite clearly formalized as 'inner world') was reconstituted along delusional lines 'not so grand but at least one in which he could live'. Bion is taking schizophrenia to be a severe consequence of the employment of projective identification and splitting of ego and objects where the attacks, under the influence of excesses of destructive impulse (perhaps connected with jealousy and envy), produce fragmentation of the personality, carrying to destruction with it the capacity for verbal thought. The consequence is that the patient in Bion's view finds himself imprisoned, not in a delusional system, but in 'a prison which seems sometimes to be me (Bion), sometimes psychoanalysis and sometimes his state of mind which is a constant struggle with his internal objects' (p. 27).

One effect is that Bion's approach is mechanistically oriented, but of course not in a mechanical cause-and-effect way but a phenomenological one. Nonetheless it must be recognized that the apostolic aspect of these papers leaves much to be desired regarding exploration of the meaning of the patient's experience in favour of exploring the mechanisms that produce the clinical phenomena. This of course is very far from the messianic Bion of later work. However, putting aside this disappointment, one can see the brilliance with which the conceptual tool of 'schizoid mechanisms' is employed by him to dissect out the phenomena. It should be noted that Bion, like Segal in her paper on 'Depression in a schizophrenic', was keen to flesh out the skeletal concepts by demonstrating how they operate in life situations, especially in the consulting room. He was not, like most workers, content to take the description of 'omnipotent phantasy' applied to splitting or projective identification as meaning that these operations occurred merely in phantasy. In fact, of course, Mrs Klein's first description of projective identification envisioned it as operative with external rather than internal objects, its latter employment only being made clear some twenty years later, as in my study of anal masturbation. If it operated with external objects, serious questions arose regarding the means by which it was brought about, the actual impact on other people, including the analyst, and the ultimate fate of split-off and projected parts of the personality.

To implement this intention Bion has made an intensive use of the countertransference, undoubtedly using the technique that he outlined in the re-view for the recognition of the operation by the patient of the mechanism of projective identification with, or really into, the analyst. But the same is true of the operation of splitting processes. He has used the countertransference and close scrutiny of the structure as well as the emotive and phantasy content of his own state of mind in response to the patient's productions, for recognition of the operation of the mechanism of splitting the object:

> The patient comes into the room, shakes me warmly by the hand, and looking piercingly into my eyes says, 'I think the sessions are not for a long while but stop me ever going out.' I know from previous experience that this patient has a grievance that the sessions are too few and that they interfere with his free time. He intended to split me by making me give two opposite interpretations at once and this was shown by his next association when he said, 'How does the lift know what to do when I press two buttons at once.' (p. 25).

This compelling example of his clinical method and mode of thought illustrates the surging creativity that Bion was trying to curb from its tendency to break out of the existing structure of psychoanalytical theory and model of the mind. But the result is a stretching of concepts to the breaking point, with attendant confusion of exposition. The existing concepts will not cover the bizarre phenomena he is trying to investigate. Thus his loyalty to Freud's position about the two principles of mental functioning and the interaction of pleasure and reality principles requires an attitude toward verbal thought which views it as being the essential instrument, the 'apparatus of awareness that Freud described as being called into activity by the demands of the reality principle' (p. 38), i.e. that consciousness was dependent upon the transformation of 'thing-representations' into 'word-representations'. Ten years later Bion will propose a more adequate tool, the concept of alpha-function. But at this time this idea of the dependence of consciousness on verbal thought gives to the schizophrenic patient's attack on his own capacity for such function a central position in the mechanics of the pathology and elbows unconscious phantasy out of the picture. The result is that splitting processes and projective identification are seen to operate on the words, as in the example of the patient splitting the word 'penis' first into its syllables and then into its component letters (p. 28), in a way that is indistinguishable from splitting of the ego that contains these functions.

The result is great confusion when Bion tries to investigate the 'bizarre objects' with which the schizophrenic's world abounds. The minute fragmentation of the apparatus of awareness and the subsequent projective identificatory expulsion of them into objects in the outside world leads at one place to their 'penetrating, or encysting, the object' and in another to their 'engulfing' the object which is then seen as if to 'swell up, so to speak, and suffuses and controls the piece of personality that engulfs it: to that extent the particle of the personality has become a thing' (p. 48), rather than the thing assuming qualities or attributes characteristic of a part of the personality. Similarly re-entry of these expelled fragments has to be explained as 'projective identification reversed'. This is meant to be different from introjection or re-introjection, but that concept too has already been stretched to the breaking point by being equated with perception, as in the description of 'the smooth introjection and assimilation of sense impressions' (p. 41). The use of these inadequate conceptual tools results in a poetry that is at once evocative and incomprehensible. For instance, when describing the state of mind in which the schizophrenic is imprisoned by the 'planetary movement' and 'menacing presence of the expelled fragments', now containing bits of objects to become 'bizarre objects', Bion writes:

> In the patient's phantasy the expelled particles of the ego lead to an independent and uncontrolled existence outside the personality, but either containing or contained by external objects, where they exercise their function as if the ordeal to which they had been subjected has served only to increase their number and to provoke their hostility to the psyche that ejected them. (p. 39).

Now clearly this way of speaking, if it is to be taken as a conceptualization rather than a poetic metaphor, is in no way compatible with Freud's model of the mind and his view of ego-functions, nor is this idea that verbal thoughts and the words they involve can be treated as things, equivalent to pieces of the personality, compatible with the view that words are ordinarily 'smoothly introjected' since introjection is a term referrable to the taking of objects into the mind. Similarly 'having thus rid himself of the apparatus of conscious awareness of internal and external reality' has not sufficient explanatory power, you might say, to account for a phenomenon such as when 'the patient achieves a state which is felt to be neither alive nor dead'. Compare it with Freud's description of Schreber's delusional system in order to grasp its conceptual pallor.

We need not labour this image of Bion's adolescent-like surge of growth bursting out of its latency-period Freudian-Kleinian clothing. But before turning to take stock of the burgeoning originality that is half stifled in these papers it is necessary to note certain rather idiosyncratic features which can be very confusing to the reader. In the first place Bion is using 'psychotic' in his differentiation from 'non-psychotic' as if it were synonymous with 'schizophrenic'. This is perhaps the consequence of his allegiance to Mrs Klein's view of the paranoid-schizoid position as the fixation point for schizophrenia. As in 'The imaginary twin' he is intent on tracing the significance of splitting processes as a concept for understanding personality structure and its phenomenology, a contribution to the development of a psychoanalytical nosology of mental disorders. The need for this was felt keenly by everyone working with psychotic patients and a notable start in this direction had already been made by Edward Glover in his well-known paper in the *Journal of Mental Science*. But Bion's use of 'psychotic part of the personality' in this way seems clearly, in its reference to splitting processes, i.e. 'part of the personality', to suggest that every psychotic part is schizophrenic. Yet the paper itself is a major contribution to establish the complexity of the disease. Mrs Klein could never have meant to include such bizarre processes as Bion is describing as part of the paranoid-schizoid position when she was considering it as a normal developmental phase of infancy and early childhood.

On the other hand it is not clear whether Bion thinks that this part of the personality is ubiquitous or only present in the person who actually presents a schizophrenic disorder. The list of predisposing personality factors: preponderance of destructive impulses, hatred of reality, unremitting dread of annihilation and premature object relations, makes it sound a quite selective disorder. This brings into view the second idiosyncratic element, namely Bion's use of the term 'reality' as in 'hatred of reality' to mean both internal as well as external reality. By this he seems to imply that there is something left over which is not hated, but one can find no reference to it, except perhaps implied in the idea that the schizophrenic exists in a state of mind that is neither alive nor dead. This is perhaps as close as he comes to indicating the delusional system as an alternative to external and psychic reality. But if the schizophrenic perhaps loves his delusional system or his 'imprisonment in a state of mind', which part of the personality wishes to escape from it? Clearly all these questions are too difficult for the conceptual framework to which Bion is being so loyal and the result is powerful descriptive poetry and conceptual confusion.

With this image of Bion's position in mind we can now turn to examine the content of his bursting originality, which finds its expression most clearly in the paper on hallucination. This paper is heavily dependent on the previous one for its conceptual framework, but the difficulty is that this framework has been worked out by an attempted compromise between Freud's concept of thinking and Mrs Klein's of unconscious phantasy. Because Bion wishes to describe and investigate phenomena which seem to imply a destruction of the patient's capacity for thought and his habitation of a world that is neither internal nor external reality, he wishes to be able to describe attacks which damage the very functions which make thought possible. This cannot be managed by the use of splitting processes and projective identification operative in an omnipotent way in relation to unconscious phantasy in Mrs Klein's sense because she has never envisioned these functions as finding discreet representation in phantasy. On the other hand Freud had no concrete conception of psychic reality that could have made use of such an idea as attack on functions, not even as late as his paper on 'Splitting of the ego in the service of defence' where he was concerned to show how illness and health can coexist in the personality.

The result is a plea for the use of 'ideographs' and 'attacks on links' as conceptual tools which is neither Kleinian nor Freudian. He will have to develop his own theory of thinking before ideas such as 'attacks on linking', extensions of the primal scene to include the 'conjunction of objects' in symbol formation or 'verbal intercourse' can become comprehensible as theory. But this is the area into which his originality in observation and thought is breaking; an area untouched by Mrs Klein and unimplemented in clinical activity by the theoretician in Freud. Just why it was that Freud paid so little attention to the implications in this direction in Schreber's memoirs is quite as mysterious as Bion's lack of reference to the same case.

It is also clear that this effort toward a theory of thinking is accompanied by dissatisfaction with the Freudian evaluation of dreams, both as regards their significance for mental life and their structure. Bion is on firmer ground than Freud in being able to consider dreams as an aspect of psychic reality, so that his grappling with the problem of the loss of reality in the schizophrenic is far less confused than Freud's attempt to differentiate between neurosis and psychosis on the basis of libido theory and withdrawal of cathexis. Bion can see that a theory of narcissism based on libido distribution or even different types of libido, or even on the later dual instinct theory will not cover. The patients he is investigating are deeply concerned with objects, but with bizarre ones whose nature he tries to describe. Conceptual attempts such as 'the unconscious would seem to be replaced by the world of dream furniture' is incomprehensible as he cannot yet give us any idea of that 'furniture', having indicated only what it isn't: 'The patient now moves not in a world of dreams, but in a world of objects which are ordinarily the furniture of dreams' (p. 40). This 'ordinarily' makes it sound a universal phenomenon of dreaming but we cannot discern what it is.

The paper on hallucination is an attempt to bring these two concepts of dream and hallucination, and at one point also the concept of delusion, into conjunction with one another: 'It is a short step from what I have already said about hallucinations to suppose that when a psychotic patient speaks of having a dream, he thinks that his perceptual apparatus is engaged in expelling something and that the dream is an evacuation from his mind strictly analogous to an evacuation from his bowels' (p. 78). In other words, he cannot bring together ordinary dreaming and hallucination because he cannot feel convinced that the dream of the psychotic is ordinary. The central idea of the paper that the process of hallucination is dependent on the use of the sense organs for the expulsion of perceived (introjected?) objects is in itself highly original. But as an idea it is probably not really new. What is new is Bion's capacity for observation of hallucinations as phenomena of the consulting room:

> When the patient glanced at me he was taking a part of me into him. It was taken into his eyes, as I later interpreted his thought to him, as if his eyes could suck something out of me. This was then removed from me, before I sat down, and expelled, again through the eyes, so that it was deposited in the righthand corner of the room where he could keep it under observation while he was lying on the couch. (p. 67)

The immense concentration which can discern small quiverings, read the meaning in a glance, note the equivocal use of language and make links with what the patient had said 'six months ago' is fairly staggering to anyone acquainted with the rigours of analytical work. This power of observation, outward and inward, is the fountainhead of Bion's originality, struggling at this time to find a conceptual framework for assembling meaningfully the masses of new observations. His loyalty to existing theory constricts him and the reader is of course deeply disappointed to find such highly novel phenomena squeezed into the constricting formulations at the end of the paper (pp. 82–85). But the clinical material is scintillating! It reveals in action the opening up of new territories of phenomenology in the consulting room which, although they seem to refer at this time to schizophrenic patients, will inevitably find representations, as yet unnoticed, in the analysis of patients of every degree of disturbance, even the 'healthy' candidate.

CHAPTER FOUR

Approach to a theory of thinking

The historical approach to Bion's work which we are following seems to reveal something of a latency period in his creativity contemporary with his apprenticeship in psychoanalysis proper, standing between the brilliance of his work with groups and the full-blown emergence of his thought in the books commencing with *Learning from Experience*. This period of reorientation was followed by the period of the papers on schizophrenia which reveal him more fully than in any other of his writings deploying his extraordinary capacity for concentration and observation. The result was his uncovering a plethora of phenomena as yet unnoticed in the consulting room, at first with frankly psychotic patients and later with the 'psychotic part of the personality' of less ill people. The consequence was a kind of adolescence of reborn creativity in which his expanding thought was struggling to stay within the bounds of existing concept, both Freud's model of thinking and Mrs Klein's model of the structure of the personality in conflict. The areas of incompatibility of the two and their fundamental inadequacy to cover the phenomena with which he was dealing was revealed in the manner in which concepts such as primal scene, splitting of the ego, projective identification and verbal thought were stretched to the breaking point.

The three papers that followed in the years straddling Mrs Klein's death in 1960 reveal the germs of the new theory. These three – 'On arrogance', 'Attacks on linking', and 'A theory of thinking – have to be read against a background of the clinical data of the earlier four in order to gain any credibility, for in themselves, very little description of the analytical situation is contained to help the reader make connections with his own experience in the consulting room. In addition the idiosyncratic features of Bion's writings are often rather exasperating: for example there is a section headed 'Curiosity, arrogance and stupidity', in which these three terms find virtually no use whatever. This stylistic aspect of Bion's writing is one which will increase rather than diminish as he goes along in the following fifteen years, making heavier and heavier demands upon the reader for an intimate knowledge of his prior works as well as an ever greater capacity to follow the high level of abstraction at which he eventually moves.

For instance, the six examples that he cites in the paper 'Attacks on linking' reveal the analytical situation in such a transcendental half-light that they seem almost a cursory obeisance to the usual technique of analytical exposition and fail to clarify the discussion following. This brings from Bion an unusual outburst of Freud-like defiant apologia: 'To some this reconstruction will appear to be unduly fanciful; to me it does not seem forced and is the reply to any who may object that too much stress is placed on the transference to the exclusion of a proper elucidation of early memories' (p. 104). This seems rather disingenuous to a reader who has been struggling to understand what he is describing when the difficulty is not the failure of 'elucidation of early memories' but rather that the 'stress – placed on the transference' is based to such a high degree on the ephemeral and 'inchoate' (and thereby indescribable) aspects of Bion's countertransference. Probably most people who have been deeply influenced in their clinical practice by Bion's work have had the same experience, of initial irritation and suspicion followed by a long period during which they have only gradually discovered the evidence of his impact on their own observations and thought. Perhaps the time will come when such an initial reaction of exasperation will seem as strange to the future reader as most people feel when informed that the first playing of a certain Beethoven quartet left the audience shocked and hostile. Certainly, for instance, the reading of the paper 'On arrogance' at the Paris congress struck many people as a shocking display of the very 'hubris' Bion was describing.

In approaching a critique of these three papers it will probably be more satisfying if we follow a sequence dictated by the internal logic of psychoanalytical theory rather than taking the papers chronologically. It is necessary to try to elucidate the moves that Bion is making to free himself from strictures on his thought. The most germinal of these is perhaps his expansion of the concept of 'part-object' beyond the bounds that could have been meant by Freud and Abraham, and used by Melanie Klein, in a concrete way, in her pursuit of the content of 'unconscious phantasy' as the premier material of the analytical situation. Bion writes: 'The conception of the part-object as analogous to an anatomical structure, encouraged by the patient's employment of concrete images as units of thought, is misleading because the part-object relationship is not with the anatomical structures only but with function, not with anatomy but with physiology, not with the breast but with feeding, poisoning, loving, hating' (p. 102).

Such an attitude seems utterly reasonable and interesting, but it is going to require an apparatus of representation quite different from that of the predominantly visual unconscious phantasy, so akin to dreaming in its composition. Bion's move to solve this problem seems to be a new concept using a deceptively old and simple word, 'link'. This is to be the unit which will be attacked or established. So the problem is moved on, so to speak, to the difficulty of discovering how the links are themselves represented. We are wondering if these links are also to be taken as the 'dream furniture' which was suggested as some thing different from the dream or dream-world: 'I employ the term "link" because I wish to discuss the patient's relationship with a function rather than with the object that subserves the function; my concern is not only with the breast, or penis, or verbal thought, but with their function of providing the link between two objects' (p. 102). We are none the wiser after this tautological statement, but rather puzzled that 'verbal thought' can be placed on the same level of conceptual abstraction as 'breast' or 'penis'.

Some clarification comes when we remember that Bion is also extending Freud's concept of the Oedipus conflict by pointing to the importance of the sphinx in the myth and suggesting that beneath the problem of incest is that of 'hubris', taken as meaning the insolent pride that is determined to discover the truth at all cost. By this extension Bion is bringing together an important gap between the thought of Freud and Mrs Klein, namely the importance of infantile curiosity, or the 'epistemophilic instinct', as she liked to call it, in the child's development. But he is also modifying her concept, which viewed curiosity as primarily directed toward the contents of the inside of the mother's body out of sadism (later specified as envy) and consequent greed, modified in the depressive position by concern about the safety of the good object. Nowhere does she, any more than Freud, despite calling it an instinct, acknowledge the thirst for knowledge as a motive in itself, seeking food for the mind. Bion comes closer to this when he speaks of 'the impulse of curiosity on which all learning depends' (p. 108).

But nonetheless Bion is able to point to a very interesting aspect of the problem of learning, the ability to ask 'why' something is taking place – in either the object, the relationship, or the state of mind – and not merely 'what' it is' (p. 102). This he identifies with questions of causality, by which, as already mentioned, he does not mean mechanical determination but phenomenological relatedness. In this sense he is thinking of mental phenomena in a way quite different from Freud's idea of 'overdetermination', which simply hedged the question of causality by multiplication of the factors into a field theory.

By this move of including the connection between baby and breast as a 'link' analogous to that between penis and vagina in the genital Oedipus conflict he has at least given a location to the prototype of what he means by link and filled it with a function at a mental level, 'learning'. But again it is stretching Mrs Klein's concept of the function of the breast relationship beyond its bounds, for in her view the functions of the breast as the prototype 'good object' were limited to its protection of the infant from the excess of persecutory anxiety engendered by the death instinct (diminished by splitting-and-idealization) which were the major threat to its achievement of integration in the depressive position.

One could therefore say that Bion has evaded, at this point, the problem of representation of linking in favour of citing the infant–breast relationship as its prototype and giving it some specific function, learning, that has a promise of including the area of 'verbal thought' by embracing 'all the perceptual apparatus including the embryonic thought which forms a link between sense impressions and consciousness' (p. 107). Here is the task which he sets himself and will try to acquit in the years to follow; the exposition and elucidation of 'embryonic thought which forms a link between sense impressions and consciousness'.

At this point he is able only to establish that thought has some connection with the developmental process and the means of communication between mother and child. Falling back on Freud's concept of introjection, the mechanics of which have always remained mysterious and virtually unexplored, and the extended concept of projective identification as described by Melanie Klein, he is at least able to investigate the failure of learning pursuant to the 'excessive' use of this latter mechanism. Unlike Mrs Klein he is not content with this quantitative statement but explores the emotive content and motivation for its employment, the 'hatred of the emotions' from which it is 'a short step to hatred of life itself' (p. 107). Here he must fall back also on the predisposing factors, in particular the excesses of death instinct, involved in the formation of the psychotic part of the personality, even though he makes real headway in defining the nature of the environmental failure, namely the failure of the mother to be able to receive and modify the infant's projection of those parts of its personality which are at the moment suffused with the fear that it is dying. Since he is still considering the paranoid-schizoid position as a 'phase of development', it is not clear when he speaks of the 'psychotic infant' whether he means to refer to the states of mind characterized by the formation of bizarre objects and their projection and re-introjection to form the 'persecutory superego' as a ubiquitous one or present only in those infants where the environmental failure is compounded by an unfortunate predisposition of temperament.

This then is the distance Bion has come in the first two papers in both locating and trying to solve the conceptual limitations of existing theory as tools for exploring the phenomena thrown up in the consulting room by the 'psychotic part of the personality'. He is viewing the whole thing as a 'disaster' which may be uncovered in the course of an analysis, a disastrous failure, that is, in the early development of the capacity for 'embryonic thought'. Out of this failure, he suggests, there arises fragmentary splitting of ego and objects and 'excessive' use of projective identification that forms a world of 'dream furniture' composed of bizarre objects and a persecutory superego which, together with the impaired capacity for thought itself, comprises the essential phenomenology of the schizophrenic disorder or of the 'psychotic part of the personality'.

In this chapter it does not seem useful to take up fully the content of the paper 'A theory of thinking' but only to view it as a preliminary statement to *Learning from Experience*. We can take stock of it to see the new moves that he is making in order to try to grapple with the problem he has recognized inherent in the phenomena he has observed. His most important move is to 'restrict' the meaning of 'consciousness' from its phenomenological sense to an operational one, following Freud's early description of it in the seventh chapter of the *Traumdeutung* as a 'sense organ for the perception of psychic qualities'. This is a Platonic view of knowledge. Whether it is to prove compatible with the more Aristotelean view of knowledge as a mating of internal expectations (Bion's pre-conceptions) with external facts (realizations) to form conceptions is a question I am not qualified to answer. But certainly it is congruent with Bion's flexible approach to sense organs and their functions as described in the paper on hallucination.

By viewing consciousness as essentially turned inward upon the self, he can then formulate the infant's mental helplessness and dependence on the mother (later on the internalized breast and mother) as primary for thinking and not merely secondary to its need for modulation of its fear of dying. This service to the infant he will call 'alpha-function' to indicate its mysteriousness. This apparatus is to be viewed as creating the elements, thoughts, which are necessary for manipulation in a process to be called 'thinking'. This is the second move, the reversal of the ordinary assumption that thoughts are the product of thinking. He is going to view them as the building blocks for constructions of thinking that will eventuate in concepts.

The third move is to bring into play concepts of omnipotence and omniscience in a meaningful, not merely a quantitative way, for he is going to view them not merely as hypertrophied functions but as qualitatively different from reason:

> If tolerance to frustration is not so great as to activate the mechanism of evasion and yet is too great to bear dominance of the reality principle, the personality develops omnipotence as a substitute for the mating of the pre-conception, or conception, with the negative realization [frustration] ...
>
> This involves the assumption of omniscience as a substitute for learning from experience by aid of thoughts and thinking. There is therefore no psychic activity to discriminate between true and false. (p. 114)

Instead there takes place a 'dictatorial affirmation that one thing is morally right and the other wrong'. We are perhaps left unclear as to whom the dictator is dictating, but the differentiation between science and morality is clear. Just how this relates to the whole area of values introduced by Mrs Klein into psychoanalysis with the concepts of paranoid-schizoid and depressive position must remain unanswered for the moment.

The final move attempts to grapple with the question 'why' which we all, as non-psychotic personalities, are supposed to be able to ask. Why is an apparatus for thinking necessary in the first place? Bion of course will tolerate no tautological or teleological argument. Instead he stuns us with: 'If the conjoined data harmonize, a sense of truth is experienced. The failure to bring about this conjunction of sense data induces a mental state of debility in the patient as if starvation of truth was somehow analogous to alimentary starvation' (p. 119). He means what he says apparently, that the mental apparatus is constructed on the model of the digestive system.

We are startled also to realize that we have come full circle (by the end of the third paper) from where we had started with the first. There we learned that Oedipus' crime was his insolent pride in being determined to know the truth at all costs. Now we learn that lack of truth-function causes a debility of mental starvation. The suspicion we must entertain and hold for the future is that the differentiating features lie somewhere in the realm of 'insolent pride' and 'dictatorial assertion'. But what this means in terms of a formalized theory of mental structure and function is difficult to see.

CHAPTER FIVE

Alpha-function and beta-elements

In the previous chapter we examined the approach to a theory of thinking that had been forced upon Bion from two directions, one coming from the torrent of new phenomena that he was observing in his application of the strict psycho-analytical method to the treatment of schizophrenic patients and the other coming from the manifest inadequacy of existing theory to cover these phenomena. By 'cover' it is not meant to convey 'explain' as much as 'organize' for the purpose of coherent description. As Bion says in *Learning from Experience*:

> It appears that our rudimentary equipment for "thinking" thoughts is adequate when the problems are associated with the inanimate, but not when the object for investigation is the phenomenon of life itself. Confronted with the complexities of the human mind, the analyst must be circumspect in following even accepted scientific method; its weakness may be closer to the weakness of psychotic thinking than superficial scrutiny would admit (p. 14).

This is very reminiscent of Freud's statement at the end of the Schreber case to the effect that there might be more similarity between his theories and Schreber's delusions than he would like to recognize.

The point about this inadequacy in our ability to think about mental phenomena is, by extension, applicable of course to the language in which it can be framed, which has, after all, been developed at the lexical level for describing the 'world' as objects in motion and in relationship, more or less as if they were purely mechanical in their principles of operation. This is the problem that Bion sets out to master in *Learning from Experience* to implement the nine moves which he had made in the previous papers in preparation for a frontal assault, so to speak, on the task of framing a theory of thinking that could really be used in the analytical consulting-room.

These nine moves, you will recall, were the following: (1) extension of the concept of part-object to include mental functions; (2) erection of the concept of 'linking' as the thing 'attacked' when the person seeks to destroy his capacity for thought and emotion; (3) extension of the Oedipus complex to include the action of 'hubris' upon the functioning of the epistemophilic instinct; (4) definition of the prototype of the linkage that generates 'learning' as the baby–breast link; (5) giving substance of a qualitative nature to Mrs Klein's idea of 'excessive' projective identification, namely the motive of 'hatred of emotions' and therefore of life itself; (6) limiting the concept of consciousness operationally, as the 'organ for the perception of psychic qualities', after Freud; (7) reversal of the usual idea that 'thinking' generates 'thoughts', so that 'thoughts' in existence require an apparatus for 'thinking' them; (8) giving a new substance to the concept of omnipotence, functioning in the realm of thought as omniscience, the 'dictatorial assertion that one thing is morally right and the other wrong'; and finally (9) the suggestion that the mental apparatus needs truth as the body requires food.

If we think of these nine as the forces he was mobilizing for his assault, we may, to follow the metaphor, consider that the key to his strategy is contained in Chapters 3–11 of *Learning*, those in which he develops the 'empty' concepts of alpha- and beta-elements and functions. It is more useful to think of these as his strategy than to mistake them for theories. That would be to misunderstand quite completely the nature of Bion's work for the next fifteen years, which is devoted to trying to fill these empty concepts with meaning. Learning is in that sense both the seminal work but also the opening skirmish of his assault, the master plan and the first attempt to implement it. Our task therefore in these two chapters is to take stock of both the progress of his assault on this mysterious fortress and the ways in which he fails to take it by storm.

His procedure may seem to you a novel one more applicable to the physical sciences, which can be mathematized, and Bion certainly had in mind, from the point of view of the philosophy of science, Mendelleyeff's achievement with the periodic table of elements as the model upon which he wished to operate. It is used again later in a more global way in the construction of the 'Grid' of the 'elements of psychoanalysis'. But in fact this is probably only a particularly self-conscious instance of the method by which psychoanalysis has proceeded in its major moves forward from the very beginning. 'Beyond the pleasure principle' posits two 'empty' concepts, life and death instincts; 'Notes on some schizoid mechanisms' does the same with splitting and projective identification. These great seminal papers were exercises in intuition to which armies of analysts have had subsequently to give substance by clinical findings derived by their use. We are still in the process of discovering what projective identification 'means', not that we assume that Mrs Klein necessarily 'meant' all that in 1946, consciously or otherwise.

So one need not be intimidated by the mathematical forms, the talk of 'functions' and 'factors' by which Bion attempts to give precision to his purpose of being as imprecise as possible. 'The term alpha-function is, intentionally, devoid of meaning – it is important that it should not be used prematurely to convey meanings, for the premature meanings may be precisely those that it is essential to exclude' (p. 3). But it is difficult, having in hand as reader all the data of earlier papers, to obey this injunction once he starts to describe the apparatus of his imagination. He wants to describe a mythical apparatus which could perform the function of processing 'emotional experiences' (which may occur in either the waking or sleeping state) in such a way as to generate 'dream thoughts' which can be stored as memory or used for thinking. He wants to imagine ways in which this mythical apparatus could go wrong, either failing to function or function in reverse, and the possible clinical consequences. So he is going to call the whatever-it-is that appears in the mind when alpha-function fails to operate by the un-name, beta-elements. Furthermore to give its consequences structural firmness he is going to imagine a continuing alpha-function turning out a membrane of thought which will function as a 'contact barrier' between conscious and unconscious, while, when it operates in reverse it will throw out a beta-screen which prevents such differentiation.

Now how are we to examine what he, Bion, means without transgressing his injunction against prematurely investing it, the concept, with meaning? Let us see if we can indeed usefully examine this mythical machinery of the mind: 'An emotional experience occurring in sleep does not differ from the emotional experience occurring during waking life in that the perceptions of the emotional experience have in both instances to be worked upon by alpha-function before they can be used for dream thoughts' (p. 6). Now he is not saying they are the same but that they do not differ insofar as they both require alpha-function, etc. in relation to the 'perception' of the emotional experience. So alpha-function does not operate on the experience but on its perception, which we learn embraces both the 'sense impressions and the emotions', 'of which the patient is aware'. The 'aware' takes us by surprise. But we must remember that he is not describing the ego, or consciousness, but has the right to assume these exist by virtue of his limiting the operational significance of consciousness to 'an organ for the perception of psychic qualities'. Apparently then alpha-function is operating on what consciousness – the organ – has perceived, awake or asleep. Well, we must have forgotten that this limiting of the concept 'consciousness' to an operational sphere implied that, of course, sleeping is not the same as being unconscious but only that the psychic qualities being perceived are mainly limited to intrapsychic events, as the organs of exteroception have (relatively) closed down for the night.

We must note for future reference, perhaps with some disappointment, that Bion is not proposing to tell us anything at this point about the emotions themselves. Clearly, unlike

Freud who in his theories persisted in treating emotions in a James-Langean way as bodily states attending the vicissitudes of instinct perceived as emotional states – essentially therefore archaic – Bion is intent on treating them as the very heart of the matter of mental life, in keeping with Mrs Klein's implications. But alpha-function is going to operate on emotions already in existence as part of the 'experience'. It may strike us as difficult to take in, this ranging side by side, as at the same level of function (or abstraction, from the point of view of exposition) of the three: sense impressions, emotion, experience. Clearly by 'impression' he does not mean 'data' in the neurophysiological sense. He may seem to be talking about processes on the border between brain and mind but he would, surely, consider this border to be marked by an unbridgeable gulf at least as wide and deep, probably wider and deeper, than that separating animate from inanimate. Presumably the 'sense impressions' are impressions of the mind operating upon sensory data already neurophysiologically ordered by all those processes studied by neurophysiologists, experimental and gestalt psychologists. We must go back to 'Groups' in order to understand Bion's meaning. The (equally empty) concept of a proto-mental apparatus included functions of the mind in which emotions and bodily states were not as yet distinguished from each other. This is borne out by the example: 'A child having the emotional experience called learning to walk is able by virtue of alpha-function to store this experience. Thoughts that had originally to be conscious become unconscious and so the child can do all the thinking needed for walking without any longer being conscious of any of it' (p. 8). He calls this 'learning a skill'. Learning, suppression and repression are thus to be linked, becoming perhaps synonymous, thus erasing the significance of the difference between the systematic unconscious and the repressed unconscious drawn by Freud in 'The ego and the id'. In this way we begin to see that the 'empty' concept of alpha-function has implications which, if found to be useful in practice, would begin to fill the empty vessel.

In fact Bion's description of the products of alpha-function (alpha-elements), that they 'resemble, and may in fact be identical with, the visual images with which we are familiar in dreams', strongly suggests that his model of the mind is going to replace

Freud's 'primary' process with 'impressions of emotional experience', and 'secondary' process with 'dream- thoughts', and thus create an entirely different approach to the analysis of dreams. It would imply that 'the elements that Freud regards as yielding their latent content when the analyst has interpreted them' would no longer have 'latent content' which had to be discovered through reversal of the 'dream work', but meaning, which would need to be understood by thinking. The vessel is filling up certainly, for many analysts would agree that they think about, rather than decode, dreams, discerning their meaning and construing their significance by a process having no resemblance at all to Freud's alleged 'jig-saw puzzle' method.

But we are leaping ahead of our intention to stay in Chapters 3–11 to try to understand what Bion means, which must be in historical context, before tracing his own attempts to fill the concept of alpha-function with clinically useful meaning. The next question that arises is: how does the model of alpha function operating on the sense impressions of emotional experience, such as learning from experience to walk, generating a continuous 'membrane' of dream thoughts which can function as a contact barrier between conscious and unconscious (both as immediate experience and as mental system) compare with Mrs Klein's and Susan Isaacs' concept of unconscious phantasy? Does it displace it to the same extent that it supersedes Freud's ideas of primary and secondary process, which, after all, he viewed as having implicit the differentiation between rational and irrational (primary process knowing nothing of negation, being timeless, etc)?

First of all it is necessary to remember that Mrs Klein was in no sense a theoretician. She was not concerned to develop a theory of the mind but was purely a descriptive clinician using Freud's model of the mind as the basis for description of the phenomena that she discovered in her playroom and consulting room. For this reason the evolution of her theories, so-called, follow a smooth line of development determined by the internal logic of discovery. At no point does she seem greatly aware of the immense changes of implicit model of the mind that her discoveries indicate. The concreteness of the inner world; the geography of mental spaces; the central role of affects; the crucial function of values – all this is an addendum to psychoanalytical theory that cannot really be contained by the basically energetics model (operating even upon the structures of ego, id and superego) suggested by Freud.

The concept of a continuous stream of unconscious phantasy in waking and sleeping states is taken as a fact not requiring explanation of its genesis. It seems implied that it is produced by mental mechanisms intrinsic to the apparatus of the mind; principally by projection and introjection, managing a commerce between the spaces of outer and inner world of objects and self. It is a great advance over Freud in that it provides, by this interaction of mechanisms, a theatre where meaning can be generated (the internal world) and thus makes this arena primary for emotional relations. We see the external world as, that is as a reflection of internal relations from the point of view of meaning and significance. There is no such apparatus in Freud's model, the distinction between pleasure and reality principles being so bound to body sensations and gratification of instinctual needs, the alternative to which is hallucinatory wish fulfillment. Primary process derives its irrationality from this purpose and any thirst for knowledge would arise only secondarily to the requirements of the reality principle. Consequently the epistemophilic instinct which Mrs Klein envisages as so important a factor in development, and which Bion will place alongside love and hate as the third great motive force in mental activity (K), could find no crucial role in Freud's model. If we take it then, historically, that the concept of unconscious phantasy superimposes itself upon that of primary process in order to allow for the development of a concrete inner world as this theatre for the generating of meaning, bound in emotionality, we can see that the phenomena of disorders of thought for which Bion was seeking a model required an additional modification. The processes of projection and introjection, even amplified by ideas of minute fragmentation, the extension of part-object concept to cover mental functions, and the idea of agglomeration of fragments to form bizarre objects, could not be used to give order to such phenomena as the existence of thoughts that could not be used for thinking, of hallucinatory phenomena and of concreteness of thought where words become things. So Bion's idea of alpha-function is intended to envisage a hypothetical function and an apparatus for performing it which could be imagined to produce both digestible and indigestible elements, assuming that the functions of the mind have been developed on the model of the experience of the functions of the alimentary canal. (It is left open, whether Bion is using this only as analogy or whether he thinks that the evolution of the mind has employed this analogy.)

From this point of view then we can say that the idea of alpha-function only seems to throw Freud's primary and secondary process out the window. As a second echelon modification, superimposed on Mrs Klein's implicit modification, it is merely a more complex model which allows for the inclusion of more complex phenomena. Freud was trying to describe the distribution of the libido and its vicissitudes, Mrs Klein was bringing these into the sphere of object relations, and Bion is attempting to account for the development of thought and learning within the confines of object relations, and thus for their pathology. By erecting an apparatus which could be imagined to function to produce thoughts that could be used for thinking he is giving substance to the word 'experience' which, as we have seen in studying the work on groups, was central to his preoccupations from the pre-analytic days of his work. The 'experienced officer'.

So we should be able to turn now to the negative aspect of the myth of alpha-function in order to understand its meaning, as an empty concept. Bion is going to use the label beta-element for those 'sense impressions of emotional experience' which are not worked upon by alpha-function. This means that he is not envisioning a beta-function in itself. Beta-elements are the raw materials of thoughts, indigestible by the mental apparatus, that cannot be stored as memory but only as accumulations of facts. He must leave it open whether such storage does in fact take place and, if so, whether this accumulated debris of emotional experiences can be recycled through the alpha-function. Now this begins to sound a lot like early Freud, in his theories of hysteria, where traumatic experiences were somehow imagined to be lodged like foreign bodies in the mental apparatus and not 'worn away' by some process that linked them with other memories. Just as, in keeping with this idea, the therapeutic process turned upon the recovery from amnesia of these events and their subsequent 'working through', we would be justified in assuming that the idea of beta-element storage as random facts would also imply a therapeutic process of their recycling for inclusion in memory.

Bion's vision includes other possibilities, in keeping with the digestive model. They may be evacuated, but where? They may be used as weapons, but how? They may be treasured and hoarded, but with what consequences? They may be recycled but without alpha-function. We are immediately struck by a similarity between these possibilities and phantasies in the sphere of anal erotism at a part-object level. But we must obey Bion's injunction against premature attribution of meaning to the mythical apparatus. Nonetheless, the immediate impression of anal phantasy does remind us that, in assessing the value of the construction, alpha-function, we must ask ourselves if it really enables a new approach to phenomena unmanageable by previous theory or is it a disguised application of existing theory to the new phenomena.

The final novelty of this apparatus, the idea of alpha-function operating in reverse, that is of its cannibalizing alpha-elements or dream-thoughts to produce beta-elements, enables Bion to double back on himself and suggest that this may be an alternative method of producing the bizarre objects he had previously accounted for by minute fragmentation and agglomeration. The mechanistic and mythic nature of his conception begins to resemble a Ronald Searle cartoon, and we begin to imagine the old machine broken down, its leaky pipes tied together with the old school tie, churning out beta-elements and filling the attic of the stately old home with unusable archaic rubble. But this impression has been created here because the clinical references have been screened out of Bion's discourse in order to bring before you the apparatus in its historic context of theory-building. In subsequent chapters it should be possible to trace the ways in which Bion fills it with clinical facts, measuring the success and failure of his first assault.

CHAPTER SIX

Container and contained: the prototype of learning

To complete our critique of *Learning from Experience* two major tasks seem to present themselves. The first of these is to build upon the description of alpha-function by examining its relation to the three functions – love (L), hate (H) and knowing (K) – which Bion selects as the three major types of emotional experiences to whose 'sense impressions' alpha-function is applied for the generating of dream-thoughts and the membrane of the contact barrier differentiating conscious and unconscious, thus making possible the binocular vision which psychoanalysis exploits in its method of study. The second would be to examine the prototype of relation-ship, namely the baby–breast as container–contained, in which learning from experience is conceived to come into existence as a possibility (phylo- and onto-genetically, one supposes), to see if Bion has succeeded in laying the foundations for a theory of the emotions for the first time in the history of psychoanalytical thought. It certainly is one of his intentions.

Before embarking on these two critical tasks it might be useful to put to one side for future consideration an aspect of the mode of presentation of the ideas in this little book which does almost universally stir every negative feeling. This is the quasi mathematical form in which the ideas are presented, with Greek letters whose names most people never knew, plus signs, dots, erotic symbols, and letters of various sorts. In Chapter Five the use of the 'empty' concept of alpha- and beta- was defended as a methodological procedure. But it was also suggested that this is an inevitable part of the movement in any science, that a theory should begin relatively empty, at least, and gather its meaning as it snowballs along – or, of course, fail to do so. That methodological fact was not seen in itself to justify the use of Greek letters. But the wish to avoid 'premature' filling of the emptiness by virtue of the employment of words for a name, which words would in themselves carry a preformed 'penumbra' of meaning from earlier usages, seemed cogent. In this field in particular it would seem to be superior to the compounding of neologisms from the Greek or to deriving names from myths.

This, however, is not the rationale for the general mathematical form in which Bion has chosen to present the main ideas of this book. That derives from an aspiration toward precision of description as the basis for precision of thought which aspires to place psychoanalysis on a footing with astronomy, say, for the purposes of intra-disciplinary communication. From that point of view *Learning* is also the prelude to *The Elements of Psychoanalysis*. Bion writes:

> As an example of an attempt at precise formulation I take alpha-function and two factors, excessive projective identification and excess of bad objects. Suppose that in the course of the analysis these two factors are obtrusive to the exclusion of other factors that the analyst has observed. If psychoanalytic theory were rationally organized it should be possible to refer to both these factors by symbols which were part of a system of reference that was applied uniformly and universally. The Kleinian theory of projective identification would be referred to by initials and a page and paragraph reference. Similarly, Freud's view of attention would be replaced by a reference. This can in fact be done, though clumsily, by reference to page and line of the Standard Edition even now. Such a statement could lend itself to mere manipulation, more or less ingenious, of symbols according to apparently arbitrary

rules. Provided that the analyst preserves a sense of the factual background to which such a formulation refers, there are advantages in the exercise in precision and rigour of thought that is exacted by an attempt to concentrate actual clinical experience so that it may be expressed in such an abstract notation. (p. 38)

This seems worth quoting at length in order to make clear that Bion is serious about the mathematical form; it is not just window-dressing to impress the uneducated. The 'mere manipulation' is stressed to make clear his vision of the kind of 'exercise in precision' that could assist in training, research, communication. This aspiration is not, certainly, to be confused with the grandiosity of Freud's early albatross, *Project for a Scientific Psychology*, but is rather comparable with the efforts of the young Wittgenstein in his *Principia Mathematica*. Perhaps we will see later if Bion gives way to contentment with phenomenological description like the later Wittgenstein of the *Philosophical Investigations*.

With this aid for setting aside our tentative irritation with Bion's method of exposition, we should be able with some calmness to examine the implications of his application of the myth of alpha-function to the three types of emotional linkages, love, hate and knowing, which are the heart of the matter of the 'emotional experiences' to whose perception the alpha-function is applied. Then we can go on to examine what he seems to be meaning by these three emotional linkages. We must remember that Bion has suggested that the digestion of emotional experiences provides the nourishment by truth which keeps the mental apparatus alive and enables it to grow by this process of learning from experience: 'Failure to use the emotional experience produces a comparable disaster in the development of the personality; I include amongst these disasters degrees of psychotic deterioration that could be described as death of the personality' (p. 42). Clearly he feels that relationships dominated by love and hate have been at the very centre of analytical investigation, particularly by Mrs Klein, and that his attention, with the view of investigation thinking processes, is mainly with K, knowing, and later Un-knowing (minus K). A3 with love and hate links, K-linkage involves mental pain which may be accepted, modified or evaded and it is naturally the latter two which concern the psychoanalyst who is trying to understand development and its pathology. The truth and the lie emerge as the food and poison of thought and growth of the personality. Historically speaking, then, Bion is going to approach the pathology of thought in a way that transforms the concept of mechanisms of defence into mechanisms for modifying the truth so that it is digestible or evading it to form the lie which is the indigestible beta-element or the bizarre object of hallucination or concrete modes of thought where words or other representations of things-in-themselves are treated as the things-themselves: 'Such a manoeuvre is intended not to affirm but to deny reality, not to represent an emotional experience but to misrepresent it to make it appear to be a fulfilment' (p. 49).

One can see that this approach involves an important amendment to the theory of reality testing which, in Freud's writing, was not given substance, was merely a fact. It is never really touched upon in Mrs Klein's work for she was concerned almost exclusively with the differentiation of the two main areas of reality, internal and external. At the time of her writing, because the phenomena being examined were those related to confusion rather than disorders of thought, her clarification of this geography of mental life seemed to give adequate substance to the problem of reality-testing. She went a great distance in demonstrating how different were the laws governing the internal and external worlds. As she was no theoretician of the mind it did not occur to her to relate this to Freud's ideas of primary and secondary process. But truly this addendum to analytical theory did not really fill out a concept of reality-testing and nowhere in her work will one find reference to any psychic entity such as a lie. Bion's myth of alpha-function is intended to provide an apparatus which can afford the personality the kind of experience from which comes a 'feeling of confidence' at discerning the truth, analogous to the confirmation of sense data by shared experience with others or confirmation by more than one sense (what Bion calls 'common sense'). This feeling of confidence, he suggests, is made possible by the elaboration of the 'membrane' of the 'contact barrier' between essentially conscious and essentially unconscious representations of the emotional experience being worked upon by alpha-function. The alpha-elements are not the experience of the thing-in-itself but an abstraction and representation of it, while its being thus represented both in conscious and unconscious forms simultaneously gives the personality a 'binocular vision' of the experience from which the 'feeling of confidence' in its reality is derived.

Now such an idea may not seem to say anything substantial until one examines its implication for reality testing. Freud's idea of thought as trial action always carried the implication that testing of the validity of the thought in action would eventually be necessary. At least it would be necessary for correct rather than erroneous ideas. Mrs Klein's introduction of the internal world distracted attention from this problem as if it did not matter, as for instance with the operation in psychic reality of omnipotent phantasies. It seemed necessary only to help the patient, for instance, to locate the operation as internal.

Bion seems to imply that it does matter, and not just from the point of view of psychic structure and mental health, but in more alarming ways that make a new sense of the psychoses as 'death of the personality'. Taking physical processes as analogy, one might say that the three theories are comparable in this way: Freud says if you do not have good sexual relations you will develop unpleasant symptoms; Mrs Klein says if you do not receive love you will develop inadequately (mental rickets); Bion says if you do not digest your experiences you will poison and destroy your mind. They are all correct theories at different levels of preoccupation with mental life. From the Freud vertex, reality-testing depends on experiences of satisfaction; from the Kleinian, on experiences of security; but from Bion's point of view reality testing depends on 'feelings of confidence' that one is seeing the truth, not of the thing-in-itself, but of one's own emotional experience of it by virtue of binocular vision: simultaneous conscious and unconscious vertices. Therefore the testing in action would not be necessary. Observation and contemplation would not only be sufficient but 'the better part', to borrow a phrase from the story of Mary and Martha. This has, as you can see, the widest implications for the theory of the psychoanalytical method, which Bion will explore later in *Attention and Interpretation*.

Having described the mythical apparatus, Bion, of course, must also give an equally mythical account of how it could possibly have come into operation, phylo- and onto-genetically. Bion's phylogenetic suggestion, which is probably not a mere analogy, is that the psychic apparatus developed alpha-function by analogy, on the basis of its observations of the function of the alimentary canal, observations which do not, of course, correspond precisely with the observations of modern physiology. From all the sense data bombarding the brain, that neurophysiological apparatus constructs an emotional experience in the mind which alpha-function swallows and sets about digesting to form alpha-elements or dream-thoughts on two levels, perhaps analogous to respiration and deglutition. That seems a tenable myth, in line with Freud's dictum that the ego is in the first instance a body ego that has evolved as a specialized function of the more primitive id.

But what of onto-genesis? Bion's myth is that the hungry or otherwise distressed baby has a pre-conception of a breast which shortly after birth meets a realization that is approximate enough to give rise to a conception of a breast. Thereafter its distress is experienced as an object, a no-breast, which it expels in various ways, mainly by screaming, along with the distressed part of its personality which contains the no-breast as a fear of dying. If the mother is able to receive this by her concern to contain the baby's projective identifications as its means of communication, her function of reverie, implemented by her own alpha-function, will denude the projected part of its distress and be able to return to the infant that part of itself it had projected, along with a present-breast to replace the no-breast. This is the K link by which the baby introjects a breast as an internal object with whose help alpha-function can become operative in the baby's mind until it is lost by virtue of the sadistic attacks described by Melanie Klein. That would be the basis for an oscillating state of being able and unable to think.

But the study of psychotics has indicated to Bion another possibility that goes beyond Mrs Klein's conception. An operation may take place by means of which the baby establishes an object which assists it to un-think, to mis-understand, to elaborate lies and hallucinations for the purpose of evading rather than modifying frustration and distress. His description is this:

> The model I construct is as follows: the infant splits off and projects its feeling of fear into the breast together with envy

and hate of the undisturbed breast. Envy precludes a commensal relationship. The breast in K would moderate the
fear component in the fear of dying that had been projected
into it and the infant in due course would re-introject a now
tolerable and consequently growth-stimulating part of its
personality. In minus K the breast is felt enviously to remove
the good or valuable element in the fear of dying and force
the worthless residue back into the infant. The infant who
started with a fear he was dying ends up by containing a
nameless dread.

The violence of emotion that is associated with Envy, and
can be one of the factors in the personality in which minus K
is in evidence, affects the projective process so that far more
than the fear of dying is projected. Indeed it is as if virtually
the whole personality was evacuated by the infant … The seri-
ousness is best conveyed by saying that the will to live, which
is necessary before there can be a fear of dying, is a part of the
goodness that the envious breast has removed. (p. 96)

He goes on to describe how such an object is experienced as a
'super'-ego that simply asserts its moral superiority, hates development and promotes un-learning and mis-understanding, etc.
It operates a function which is the reverse of alpha-function: 'In
other words alpha-elements however obtained, are acquired for
conversion into beta-elements' (p. 98).

All this is the mythology which Bion hopes he and other
analysts may be able in time to fill with meaning. In order to
make it more real, a piece of clinical material to illustrate the
theory in action might be helpful. Before ending this chapter
a word is necessary concerning a question raised at the beginning of the chapter. Has Bion succeeded in constructing a theory
of the mind which will lend itself to a substantial concept of
emotions that will distinguish modern psychoanalysis from other
psychologies, including Freud's, where the emotions are either
primitive anlage, noises in the machine, or bodily manifestations
of mental states perceived as emotions? Here are his statements
about it from Chapter 27:

Container and contained are susceptible of conjunction and
permeation by emotion. Thus conjoined or permeated or

both they change in a manner usually described as growth. When disjoined or denuded of emotion they diminish in vitality, that is, approximate to inanimate objects' (p. 90).

...

It is evident that we need to know what emotions are compatible with a commensal relationship and therefore with K

...

On the replacement of one emotion ... by another emotion does the capacity for re-formation, and therefore receptivity [of the container, mother, breast, etc] depend ...

Learning depends on the capacity for the (growing container) to remain integrated and yet lose rigidity. This is the foundation of the state of mind of the individual who can retain his knowledge and experience and yet be prepared to reconstrue past experience in a manner that enables him to be receptive of a new idea ...

[Container and contained] must be held by a constant [emotion] that is capable of replacement ...' (p. 93)

It seems reasonable to suggest that this is the first cogent statement of a theory of emotions in the history of psychoanalysis. It places emotion at the very centre of mental growth through learning from experience, which Bion rightly distinguishes from learning 'about' things and will greatly elaborate upon in *Transformations*.

Note
A piece of clinical material intended to illustrate the theory in action can be found in the Appendix to this book.

CHAPTER SEVEN

The elements of psychoanalysis and psychoanalytical objects

In following the evolution of Bion's thought it has gradually become apparent that he has been pursuing a vision of
refining and extending the model of the mind, as drawn up
explicitly by Freud and modified implicitly by Melanie Klein,
so that it might be used as an instrument for investigating
disturbances of thought. Such a vision of course includes the
possibility of using the psychoanalytical method, so akin to the
clinical medical method, for examining pathology for the sake
of forming hypotheses about healthy structure and function.
Added to this, peculiarly Bionic, one might say, is the interest
in formulating matters of the mind in a way that will allow
for precision of communication and 'mere manipulation' by
'arbitrary rules' in what he calls variously 'meditative review'
and the 'psychoanalytic game' (pp. 99 and 101). This duality
of aim makes the present work dual in its essential nature, half
scientific, i.e. towards the construction of a scientific deductive system, and half philosophic, i.e. investigating the system
as a thing-in-itself. It seems unlikely that this joy in 'mere
manipulation' would be a widespread phenomenon among
practising analysts and it may not be amiss if its discussion is

rather neglected here in our critique of the Grid, taking it as a method of exposition rather than an instrument meant for use. Our task in this chapter must be mainly to investigate the grid as the periodic table of psychoanalytical elements and then to trace its implications for the comprehension of what Bion calls the 'molecules' of psychoanalysis, psychoanalytical objects and interpretations. Having already constructed an apparatus, mythical and empty, namely alpha-function, which can operate on the sense impressions of emotional experiences to produce thoughts which can be used for thinking, Bion must now turn his attention to constructing an equally mythic and empty apparatus for manipulating these thoughts in a manner worthy of the name 'thinking' and capable of producing 'truth', the food of the mind. A daunting task!

This he attempts to do by drawing up his periodic table of elements, abstracting from it his molecules of psychoanalytic objects and then investigating the mechanisms, paranoid schizoid and depressive positions and projective identification (modified and represented as Ps↔D and container–contained ♀ ♂) by whose operation these molecules interact with one another. Clearly if the digestive system was the model and analogy behind the construction of the apparatus of alpha function, chemistry is the model and analogy for the grid of elements, the description of psychoanalytic objects and the investigation of their behaviour with one another under the 'causal' influence of Ps↔D and ♀ ♂. Somehow the digestive system model was in itself infused with life and also lent itself to the phylo-genetic and onto-genetic conception of how the apparatus for alpha-function could have arisen. A chemical model will have neither of these inherent virtues and we must see if Bion is able to breath the life of emotionality and growth into it and to present a cogent description of how such a system might have arisen. We need not, at this point in the history of his ideas, expect him to fill the empty vessels with a great deal more clinical meaning than is absolutely necessary for the purpose of exposition. And surely such clinical reference is thin on the ground in this book, making some chapters fairly incomprehensible on first reading, cf. Chapter 9. It must be left open whether the method of expo-sition, i.e. using letters and signs of the Grid itself, does in any

way facilitate the abstractness and emptiness of the various hypothetical apparatuses that Bion is trying to construct or whether it
merely imposes an additional and sometimes impossible task of
translation (certainly open to error) upon the reader.

Perhaps it would be worthwhile to remember the history of
the periodic table which is Bion's model. In the mid-19th century
Mendelleyeff and others discovered that by comparing atomic
weights, valency and chemical properties, chemical elements
could be arranged periodically in a nine-tiered table. Only later
was it realized that this was based upon the internal structure of
atoms, with their nuclei and circling rings of electrons. The two
axes of this table therefore originally had no structural significance and could only be designated by nine columns O–VIII.
Therefore the history of its use passed from descriptive classification (weight, valency and properties of combination) to structural delineation (electrons, protons, rings etc).

Bion's Grid is being structured in exactly the opposite way.
He has drawn up a table by designating the meaning of each
column in his vertical and horizontal axes for the sake of defining hypothetical elements (say D4, pre-conception-attention)
whose realization in clinical phenomenology could then be
sought. It is true that the Periodic Table did function somewhat
in this way, for the empty spaces in its original description did
point the way to the discovery of new elements to fill these
voids. So our first problem is to examine the means by which
Bion fixed upon the units of the two axes, the horizontal axis
(1–6) of use and the vertical axis (A–H) of genesis of thought.
In order to do this we must remember that the whole justification for it is Bion's contention that mere description 'of what
took place' (i.e. in the consulting room) is neither a 'factual
account' nor a 'scientific deductive system' but bangs somewhere in the middle and thus stands as does the 'ideogram' to
phonetic alphabet 'words'. The imputation of cumbersomeness
may seem irrelevant when we remember a contrary dictum, 'a
picture is worth a thousand words'. The Grid may be a wild-
goose chase, as is strongly suggested in Chapter 19 when Bion
tries to adapt the whole apparatus to dealing with 'feeling'
rather than 'thinking'. But there is something rather marvellous
about it as a method of exposition.

This exposition rests upon the choice of categories, both for the axes themselves (use and genesis) and the components of them: 'The choice of axes may appear arbitrary without, further reasons; it stems from the analytic situation itself' (p. 91). But be is very explicit in his expectations of the elements, their criteria of reality adequacy and capability of articulation to form a scientific deductive system, (p. 3). It therefore becomes extremely confusing when he begins to describe ♀ ♂ as an element, along with Ps↔D, LHK, R (reason) and I (idea, or psychoanalytic object) when he later calls them mechanisms (♀ ♂ and Ps↔D) or earlier had called them factors in a function (LHK). This is made even more confusing when he seems to discard ♀ ♂ as an element in favour of a 'central abstraction' which it must contain or imply, to which the term 'element' should be applied and reaches the conclusion that elements are essentially unobservable.

It is difficult to see how this conforms to the earlier expectation that elements 'must be capable of representing a realization that they were originally used to describe'. Even worse when he tries to explain that 'it will have the same status and quality as the object we aspire to *represent* by the word "line" or a line drawn upon paper, has to the word "line" or a line drawn upon paper' when there is no such object in external reality other than its representation. This breakdown of direct observability seems to explode the chemical analogy from the point of view of scientific method. His recourse to 'common sense' as he had formulated it in *Learning* does not suffice when he wants to make the further step of defining the 'dimensions' of these elements and he pleads for forbearance: 'Implementation of this plan seems, as so often in the case of psychoanalytic investigation, to presuppose what we wish to discover. In writing this I have to start somewhere and this produces difficulties because the start of a discussion tends to impose an appearance of reality on the idea that the matter discussed has a start' (p. 11). The upshot is for Bion to hook the 'premises' of psychoanalysis firmly to those of philosophy and theology, which seems to make nonsense of the aspiration toward a 'scientific deductive system'. This capitulation makes it easier to accept the 'dimensions' of sense, myth (or model making) and passion (or LHK with intensity but without violence), as tentative intuitions. It is analogous to an intuition in a 19th-century

chemist that elements of chemistry must have structural components in some dynamic relation to one another, with weight,
charge, motion, having as yet no means for observing evidences
to suggest definitive realities such as electrons, protons, orbits,
velocities. But neither the definition of the requirements nor the
dimensions of the elements explains the leap to the Grid and
its arbitrary axes, use (in a passionate two-or-more person relation) and genesis (of thought). Why it is that a cross-indexing
of use and genesis should define the qualities of the elements is
left quite mysterious. The order in the genetic axis is manifestly
logical, as the term 'genetic' implies, but that of the horizontal
'use' axis seems utterly arbitrary. Yet Chapters 8–9 suggest also a
necessary logical order. It is also difficult to see an intrinsic difference, for instance, between 'definatory hypothesis' and 'notation'
or to recognize that 'attention' and 'action' are terms at the same
level of abstraction.

In the vertical (genetic, i.e. logical series in the genesis of
thought) axis we meet again in somewhat expanded form the
formulations first exposed in the paper on thinking and the book
Learning. We must note the differences, however, in order to
understand the contribution to his theory that the arrangement
in the Grid implies. One addendum is the suggestion that beta
and alpha-elements are not only hypothetical but intrinsically
unobservable in case they do exist. So it now appears that an
alpha-element is not in itself a dream thought, for whose definition Bion returns to Freud's hypothesis of latent content. This
raises doubt about the meaning of 'observable' for certainly the
manifest content may be observable but not the latent, not even
in one's own dream, let alone another person's. It is question-
able whether one can say that the patient's dream, rather than his
account of his dream, is observable to the analyst.

The second addendum, which opens up the possibility of
mobility within the Grid, is the modification of the concept
'pre-conception' as a 'state of mind adapted to receive a restricted
range of phenomena' (i.e. part of the innate equipment of the
mind) to include the idea that 'the conception can however then
be *employed as* [my italics] a preconception in that it can express
[or does he mean 'contain'] an expectation.' He does not help
us much with the transition to 'concept' by telling us that it is

achieved 'by a process designed to render it free of those elements that would unfit it to be a tool in the elucidation or expression of truth', as if it were a chisel with a burr on its cutting edge.

All in all the components of the two axes of the Grid owe virtually nothing to existing psychoanalytic theory but owe their origins to philosophy, their lineage being only slightly indicated by Bion (cf. Kant, Poincaré, Braithwaite, Hume). It is highly original and cannot sustain itself by the respectability of its genesis. It must stand or fall on its own merits. It is not possible to pass on to examine the meaning of the Grid itself without a note of exasperated incomprehension. It must be presumed that in using the Greek letter psi (Ψ) to represent both horizontal column 2 (denial of the unknown) and also to represent the saturated element in a preconception, Bion means to imply something that he never spells out. It must be supposed that he means that the use involved is accomplished through the use of a pre-conception as if it were a conception and did not require any mating with a realization to become operative.

One other note. Because of the difficulty of the book it is impossible without consulting Bion personally (which must eventually be done) to be sure about the many apparent printer's errors (it must have been entirely incomprehensible to the poor proofreader). Page 28, for instance: line 4, the figure 5.1 must surely be rather A5. Further down, the statement 'A state of attention, being receptive to the material the patient is producing, approximates to a pre-conception and therefore the change from attention to preconception is represented by a move from D4 on the grid to E4.' This should surely read: 'A state of attention, being receptive to the material the patient is producing, functions as a pre-conception (D4) and will change to a conception (E4)', i.e. when the material arrives. In its original form the word 'pre-conception' should surely read 'change from attention to conception', although even that is unclear.

But passing on to consider the Grid itself we soon realize that it is an extraordinarily graphic way of representing the necessary movement of thoughts as they progress through the hypothetical apparatus for thinking that Bion wishes to construct. It is, to go back to the chemical analogy, akin to the chemical flowsheet which is to be used as the basis for constructing an actual chemical plant that will in fact transform certain raw materials into certain desired products and by-products. In this way it is quite different from a periodic table unless you were a modern-day alchemist who wanted to turn hydrogen into plutonium. Here the brilliance with which Bion is able to use observations on extremes of psychopathology for drawing forth implications regarding healthy functioning becomes apparent once more, but the difficulty of following the argument is daunting.

Basically the apparatus consists of concrete equipment, container–contained ($\female$ $\male$) and a dynamic influence (also called a mechanism for some reason), paranoid-schizoid and depressive positions in the sense of Melanie Klein, plus selected fact (equivalent, perhaps, to catalyst) in the sense of Poincaré (Ps↔D). The prototype model is the interaction of baby in distress and present breast. When the contained has been enveloped by the container so that alpha-function may ensue, the contained is imagined to be operated upon by Ps↔D in such a way that a process of growth ensues which can be represented on the Grid. This movement on the Grid is from left to right and from above downward as the contained thought progresses in the sophistication of both its use and its level of abstraction and organization. Ideally, one might say, what starts as beta-element ends as scientific deductive system in action (G6?). The vision is in a way similar to the view of personality proposed by Roger Money-Kyrle in which the evolution of concepts forms a pyramidal structure based on internal logical necessity ('Cognitive development', 1968).

All that is imaginative and mythical but fairly clear. We come to difficulty when we try to understand why Bion views progress from left to right in use by virtue of the mechanism container-contained and the dynamic operation of L, H, and K, to differ from movement from above to below in sophistication and level of abstraction by the operation of Ps↔D and why he calls Ps↔D a mechanism infused also with the dynamic of L, H and K. Partly the answer lies in Bion's understanding Melanie Klein's formulations as structural ones: 'The process of change from one category represented in the grid to another may be described as disintegration and reintegration, Ps↔D' (p. 35). It might be suggested that this mistakes Mrs Klein's description of the consequences of the mechanisms, such as splitting processes, employed in the two positions, for the essences of the positions themselves. But it seems clear that her ultimate use of the term 'position' was essentially an economic one, intended to focus on the central value attitude dominant in the interaction of self and objects.

This is not a criticism of Bion but a reminder that Ps↔D has reference to Mrs Klein's concepts but is not merely a short hand notation for them. It is possible that in stressing the structural implications, disintegration-integration, at the expense of value attitudes, Bion has posed himself an unnecessary difficulty. This takes the form of his having to distinguish between the 'development of thoughts', A1 to G6 on the grid, and the 'use of thoughts' under the 'exigencies of reality, be it psychic reality or external reality' when 'the primitive mechanisms have to be endowed with capacities for precision demanded by the need for survival'. He has to propose a new function, Reason with a capital R, which seems to drag him back to Freud's picture of the plight of the ego serving three masters, as represented in 'The ego and the id'. This brings us to Chapter 9 which is the heart of the book, and a gnarled heart of oak it is.

The central problem is expressed in this way: 'The operation Ps↔D is responsible for revealing the relationship of "thoughts" already created by $♀ ♂$. But in fact it seems as if Ps↔D is as much the begetter of thoughts as $♀ ♂$' (p. 37). To examine it Bion brings in outline a case in which the patient's speech was incomprehensible, equivalent to doodling, but was somehow able to invest the objects of the room, presumably including the analyst, with meaning that had no connection with their forms or functions. Bion says he was using these objects as 'signs', probably equivalent to what Hanna Segal has called 'symbolic equations', rather than symbols. This seems to be the same as psi (Ψ), column 2, or the pre-conception used as if it were already saturated by a realization to form a conception. This would seem to relate to omniscience, confabulation, lying, minus K. The patient was thus mistaking a notational system for symbols and metaphors and trying to think with this inadequate equipment. But Bion sees it as, at least, an attempt to liberate himself from having to manipulate actual objects in order to think. In this way it would seem to have the same relation to thought as play has to phantasy. But Bion thought he could also detect that the patient was attempting to use one particular object to harmonize and give a pattern of meaning to the others, analogous to the function of the selected fact, but of course employed concretely as a beta-element, as a thing-in-itself. One has to stretch the imagination to grasp the gossamer description of the clinical phenomena, but we must take Bion's intuitions of the facts on trust.

What he deduces from this is confrontation with a chicken and-egg problem: which comes first, Ps↔D or container? This may seem a bit of his 'mere manipulation by arbitrary rules of logic' but the leap that he takes from it is impressive: 'I shall suppose the existence of a mixed state in which the patient is persecuted by feelings of depression and depressed by feelings of persecution. These feelings are indistinguishable from bodily sensations and what might, in the light of later capacity for discrimination, be described as things-in-themselves. In short beta-elements are objects compounded of things-in-themselves, feelings of depression-persecution and guilt and therefore aspects of personality linked by a sense of catastrophe' (p. 39). It will be another five years before he can clarify this in the paper on 'Catastrophic change'. But the immediate use which Bion makes of this sense of catastrophe inherent in the beta element is dazzling. He imagines a primitive situation in which the dispersed beta-elements (which he will soon call an 'uncertainty cloud' suggestive of the theological concept of the 'cloud of unknowing'), seeking a container, are compressed by this search to form an 'abortive prototype' of the contained which is able to use the dispersed state as a 'loose-knit container'. This process would realize an equally abortive prototype of Ps↔D (taken as fragmentation–integration plus selected fact).

The question must arise: has Bion by this feat of mental and linguistic gymnastics satisfied the second requirement for an hypothesis of a mental apparatus: namely to suggest a possible way in which it could have arisen phylo- and onto-genetically? The poetry is compelling and the description of its implications, of greedy beta-elements full of a sense of catastrophe searching wildly for a saturating realization in the absence of the container (breast), is hair-raisingly real. But is it convincing compared with Melanie Klein's description of the events precipitating the onset of the depressive position? How does it compare with the description of the formation of concepts of mental spaces outlined in *Explorations in Autism*? Discussion of these questions should probably wait until we have considered the rest of the book with its investigation of psychoanalytic objects and their dimensions of sensa, myth and passion.

CHAPTER EIGHT

The role of myth in the employment of thoughts

In the previous chapter an attempt was made to describe and examine Bion's effort in *The Elements of Psychoanalysis* to imagine an apparatus capable of generating thoughts and producing growth in them in the direction of sophistication in both the level of abstraction and of organization. This he has given graphic representation by means of the Grid, where the possibility of growth in use and level of abstraction and organization is represented in a two-axis system, movement within which is conceived to be implemented by two mechanisms: container–contained (♀ ♂) and paranoid-schizoid and depressive positions, plus selected fact (Ps↔D). He also attempted to give a cogent description of how such a system could have come into existence in the species and in the individual, using a quasi-astronomical model of the 'uncertainty cloud' and the 'loose reticulum'. It was suggested that by thus emphasizing a structural metaphor and omitting the economic aspect related to emotional attitude towards value inherent in Mrs Klein's formulation of 'positions', he was setting himself an unnecessarily difficult task in regard to the 'employment' of thoughts in thinking, as contrasted with the problem of the 'manufacture' and 'growth' of thoughts. It was suggested that Bion's proposed model might be compared with Mrs Klein's description of the events which usher in the depressive position or the examination of the origin of the conception of psychic spaces as outlined in *Explorations in Autism* (Meltzer et al, 1975). We must now move on to consider the way in which Bion's apparatus is imagined to function to 'employ' thoughts and how this is seen to relate to the psychoanalytical situation and method. It should be emphasized again that in this discussion the Grid is being treated only as a method of exposition and not as a thing meant for use in 'meditative review' or 'the psychoanalytic game'.

In order to approach this problem of 'employment' of thoughts Bion has proposed, intuitively, that the 'elements' of thought must come together in a tripartite form involving sensa (row B, alpha-elements), myth (row C) and passion (LHK with intensity but without violence, but also identified as row G, scientific deductive system) to form 'psychoanalytical objects' whose contemplation may give rise to other psychoanalytic objects, interpretations. He is going to assume that in the realm of myth the human species has evolved certain trends in preconception which, though essentially private to the individual, find certain approximations in the group. The Oedipus myth is one of these, particularly with relation to problems of love and hate in the infant, while the myths of the Tree of Knowledge of Good and Evil and of the Tower of Babel may be taken as examples in the realm of K, knowledge and communication. He says: 'the myth by virtue of its narrative form binds the various components in the story in a manner analogous to the fixation of the elements of a scientific deductive system by their inclusion in the system' (p. 45). This is seen as essentially a process of nomination or naming (column 3) which leaves the work of filling with meaning still to be done. The myth 'fixes' the elements in their appropriate relation to one another but does not assign their meaning. This must be done by interpretation of the myth, which would, however, be impossible if the myth did not 'fix' the relationships. This 'system' he calls a 'moral system' (p. 46). In so far as the dream can be taken as a 'private' myth its significance for the individual can be investigated by using the 'public' myth, such as the Oedipus myth. But in the individual's 'employment' of thoughts, once his thought has progressed in its 'growth' to take the form of a dream-private-myth that 'fixes' its components in relationship to one another, it may then be used as a preconception to seek a realization in external or internal reality. This process necessarily involves mental pain, and in Chapters 11–14 Bion is at his most brilliant in demonstrating, by way of his idea of reversible perspective, one of the many ways in which pain may be so evaded that a static situation results in the growth of the thought. As a consequence no learning can occur.

It is not possible to be absolutely certain that Bion means that mental pain arises at that point in growth of a thought where it becomes fixed in dream-myth, but if this is so it would be his major contribution to a theory of affects, which is so absent in the body of psychoanalytic theory. But of course it does not go very far in investigating the nature of mental pain; it merely locates its point of origin. Yet it is certain that the problem of pain is central to the reasons for Bion calling the myth an integral part of a 'moral system'. While he does not dismiss the view that by resolving conflicts an analysis may be said to diminish suffering, he is quite firm in placing as a more central aim the increase of the patient's 'capacity for suffering' (p. 62). This capacity seems bound up with the ability to recognize emotions in their premonitory state 'before they become *painfully* obvious'; the premonition of feelings being in an analogous state *vis à vis* emotions as pre-conceptions are to conceptions in the realm of ideas. Anxiety would be closely related to this premonitory state of the emotions, in keeping with Freud's signal theory of anxiety as eventually described in 'Inhibition, symptom and anxiety', and gives a new cogency to the old dictum that analysis must be conducted in a state of deprivation if the premonitory states are to be recognizable through the suspension of action and gratification.

If this is Bion's meaning, that emotions in a premonitory state (that is, belonging to a thought that has grown into a dream-myth which is functioning as a preconception searching for a realization) manifest themselves as anxiety, the implication would be that the painfulness of the anxiety is closely bound to the uncertainty of finding a realization which would make the emotion extant rather than premonitory, '*painfully* obvious'. We can therefore assume that Bion is talking of mental pain as being of two sorts: anxiety (by which he must mean both persecutory and depressive, perhaps also confusional and catastrophic) which is related to the premonition of emotion, and other realized emotions which are in their nature painful. This would go some distance to harmonize Freud's 'signal' theory of anxiety with Mrs Klein's classification of mental pains as persecutory and depressive, both being bound to unconscious phantasy. But it also goes further by allowing for this differentiation between painful emotions and mental pain proper, anxiety. There is good reason to believe that the former, painful emotions, are rendered unbearable by their admixture with mental pain and that the efficacy of the psychoanalytical method is at least in part the result of teasing apart these categories of pain.

The next step in this preliminary skirmishing, before an assault on the problem of the employment of thought in thinking, is for Bion to link emotional and ideational 'content' of thoughts. This he does by demonstrating that the Grid categories can be just as well used for 'feeling' as 'idea' where 'feeling' is taken to be the premonitory emotion associated with an idea which is bound in the dream-myth, functioning as a preconception. Note that these are the anxieties and not the variants of L, H and K as they suffuse the emotional experience whose perception is the object of alpha-function. Having the experiences, having the emotions which are implicit in the experiences, is different from observing and thinking about the experiences. It is this latter with which Bion is concerned. In order for this 'thinking about' to take place, the experiences must become suffused with meaning. Growth of the ideas and emotions, as graphically represented by the Grid, is meant to take place in terms of their suffusion with meaning which can grow in complexity, sophistication and level of abstraction, or, if need be, as for instance when new experiences must be distinguished from old ones, shrink to naiveté. This incidentally enables him to place within the Grid a host of pathological emotional experiences which are bizarre and can be likened in the realm of emotion to beta-elements in the realm of ideas. Their realization in work with psychotic patients is legion and defies communication by any means other than projective identifications to which few analysts could expect to be receptive.

Where then does this all take Bion in the final assault? The upshot is the conception of psychoanalytical objects, loaded with the meaning of phantasy, emotion and anxiety, which the analyst can hope to reflect by producing his own psychoanalytical object – the interpretation:

> To the analytic observer the material must appear as a number of discrete particles unrelated and incoherent (Ps↔D) … The coherence that these facts have in the patient's mind is not relevant to the analyst's problem. His problem – I describe it in stages – is to ignore that coherence so that he is confronted by the incoherence and experiences incomprehension of what is presented to him' … This state must endure – until a new coherence emerges; at this point he has reached →D, the stage analogous to nomination or "binding". From this point his own processes can be represented by ♀ ♂– the development of meaning. (p. 102)

This development of meaning is seen to be aided by the mythology of psychoanalytical theory which the analyst utilizes to give coherence, point and precision to the private myths thrown up by his intuition of the transference situation. These psychoanalytical objects, the 'molecules' of psychoanalysis, are seen to be compounded of elements from three rows of the Grid – B, C and G – that is, the sensa or alpha elements which have been derived from the perception of the emotional experience, the myth or dream thought in which its elements are bound, and the passion or scientific deductive system into which it would grow if allowed. Is the citadel taken? Has Bion done anything more than 'presuppose what he wished to discover'? He ends defining psychoanalytic objects in terms of the Grid categories – which were themselves arbitrary, one might insist.

Let us assume that the citadel is not taken, that Bion has not succeeded in finding a method for teasing out the elements that are compounded in thought and therefore in the meeting of minds which is supposed to take place in psychoanalysis. The Grid does not really seem a useful instrument for 'meditative review', the axes of use and growth do not seem to define elements of discrete use-growth quality in any way analogous to the periodic table in chemistry; the tripartite 'molecules' do not immediately suggest clinical realizations; the essential role he assigns to 'naming' for processes of thought is immediately refuted by the non-literary arts and crafts, games and non-verbal modes of communication. Where does the question of 'perspective' fit into the system, if he is to claim that reversible perspective can be used to interfere with it? Let us take the stand that the book is a failure, a hodge-podge of inadequately worked out intuitions compounded from philosophy, mathematics and clinical experience and harnessed to a grandiose vision of precision, perhaps worse, of scientific respectability. Let us subject it to a merciless rejection because of its clotted language, repetitiveness, vague allusiveness, typo-graphical errors and linguistic idiosyncracy. Let us do all that and see what remains and whether we want to bother with the next book written by this fellow.

To begin, one must remember that from *Learning* onward Bion has set himself a mammoth task and we must watch with patience and suspended judgment as he pursues his way. Thus *Elements* should be assessed as a battle preceded by skirmish-ing and not as a war. Has some territory been wrested from the 'formless infinite' of the mysterious realm of mental functions? Has reading this book been an unforgettable experience that has opened vistas of thought that one could never have formu-lated for oneself? Framed thus, and allowing all the reservations mentioned above, there can be no question about the answer. But what are these vistas? Bion has framed for us a hypothetical apparatus that is capable of generating thoughts that can be used for thinking, which he now proposes to study. This process he divided into two stages: the growth of the elements of thought and the employment of these elements as objects of thought. Let us consider them separately and then try to unite them in a critical way.

The whole realm of thoughts and thinking, as against emotional responses, phantasy and conflict, is a new area to psychoanalytical investigation, opened up by Bion and explored thus far almost single-handed. The ideas Bion brings from math-ematics and philosophy defy scholastic classification and are his own personal integration of concepts taken from various sources and passed through the filter of psychoanalytical experience. Many may be aware of concepts such as level of abstraction, notation, publication, etc but it is a feat of imagination to divide thoughts on the basis of co-determination by growth in abstract level and organization linked to use. It gives a certain structural substance to the idea of a 'thought' as a mental product which gives cogency to the view that thoughts are initially empty and must be filled with meaning. Thus the whole view of preconception and 'pre-'conception mating with realization to form conception, with each level of growth in a thought functioning as the pre-conception for its next elevation in level of abstraction and sophistication of organization, brings alive the realm of thought in the way that Freud, and Abraham's stages in the development of the libido, brought the idea of psychosexual maturation to life. One need neither believe it nor grasp it fully to recognize that it is a rather glorious vision, deserving of comparison with the periodic table even if the comparison is inexact. That the concept 'container' means essentially 'container of meaning' makes a link to Mrs Klein's concept of spaces in a way that enriches the concreteness which was perhaps her greatest contribution to our model of the mind: the concreteness of psychic reality. Not only are internal objects concrete in their existence as structures of the mind but this concreteness is necessary in order for them to be able to function as containers of meaning. This concreteness of structure must be well-caulked, guarded by continent sphincters, if they are to perform their functions in the mind and provide the basis through identification for the self to become an adequate container of objects, states of mind, emotion. The link to Mrs Bick's work on skin-container function and of the group which explored the evolution of concepts of spaces in autistic children is unmistakeable.

Thus Bion's idea of the way in which paranoid-schizoid and depressive positions function as mechanisms within the container–contained structure to allow the contained thoughts to grow in complexity and accrue meaning in this process takes Mrs Klein's concept out of its Freudian framework. The 'positions' change from being massive developmental moves and became components of moment-to-moment function. It may still be contended that by dealing with Ps↔D as mechanism rather than as economic principle, by making it thus fairly indistinguishable from container–contained, by depriving it of its reference to value attitudes, Bion has greatly weakened his argument. It is equivalent to earlier days in chemistry when the catalysts were chosen on a purely chance basis since nothing was known of their mode of impingement on the chemical reaction proper. Ps↔D plus selected fact is a bit like selenium in a Keldohl flask: it is there because it works. But this omission of the economic aspect of Mrs Klein's concepts is in keeping with the mathematized effort at rigour which characterizes this book, for it will be noticed that the Grid has no place for 'aesthetic', either in use or growth. Perhaps it should come after 'algebraic calculus' as the ultimate level of growth in abstraction and sophistication. His own concept of 'attacks on linking' and the value attitudes involved should have prevented him from equating Ps↔D with disintegration–integration.

When we move on to his handling of the problem of employment of thoughts, we must first acknowledge that this distinction between growth and employment seems confusing when juxtaposed to growth and use. Perhaps he has not made clear enough that by 'use' he means the immediate context in which the thought has its genesis, while by 'employment' he means something very special – namely the capacity of the mind to understand itself, and thereby the possibility to understand other minds. He formulates this possibility in terms of 'psychoanalytical objects': the molecules of psychanalytical study, the understandings that can become available when the observable elements of thought are brought together. The requisite categories of elements, rows B, C and G (also called sensa, myth and passion) which must combine to form this molecule of understanding is intuited by Bion and nowhere justified or explained. For this reason the chapter on 'Transference' is relatively empty, the chapters on pain are fascinating but lack integration with the rest of the book, the exploration of the Oedipal, Babel and Eden myths is tangential. How Bion equates 'passion' with 'scientific deductive system' is a mystery. One must conclude that he means something like: in order for the thought to grow to a level where it can take its place in a scientific deductive system it must have been apprehended and worked upon in the course of its development in the container by Ps↔D operating with LHK, intensely but without violence. That could lead to a new approach to problems of creativity.

Certainly the idea that in psychoanalysis we are studying 'objects' causes a linguistic muddle of the type that Bion has been explicitly at great pains to avoid, yet often violates unnecessarily, as for instance in his various uses of the word 'element'. But perhaps he does somehow mean that his 'psychoanalytical objects' are the very stuff of which the 'objects' of 'object relations' are made. At any rate, by giving such a detailed analysis and synthesis of thought he has offered a new firmness for the much abused and thus unbearably vague term 'understand' when applied to states of mind, one's own and those of others.

All in all one has to say that *The Elements of Psychoanalysis* is a glorious failure, glorious in its vision and scope of thought and a failure in its organization and hobby-horsishness.

Psychoanalytical observation and the theory of transformations

It was suggested in the chapters dealing with the *Elements* that Bion might be viewed from a rather military model as mustering forces, making sallies and skirmishes and periodically trying to take the citadel of the mind by storm. Perhaps this is too sanguinary a model to account for the experience of the reader who finds himself in a near constant state of exasperation eased by moments of delight and illumination. Perhaps we should imagine a present-day Leonardo designing his flying machines and incidentally producing marvellous drawings and paintings and entertaining fireworks shows and mechanical toys. Perhaps our exasperation will be less if we put to one side the desire to see him fly (or crash?) and enjoy the art and fireworks. To do that requires no critical guidance. *Transformations* has some masterpieces of clinical description, notably the twofold description of Patient B (p. 19), and sparkles throughout with little fireworks of observation and thought about the psychoanalytical situation and the world it inhabits. But our task in this book is to take Bion's main purpose seriously and to struggle with our resentment, suspicions that he is mad, feelings of humiliation at his citing authors whose work is hardly known to us as if it were as current as the news on TV, and above all exasperation with the mathematizing. He says explicitly that he rejects the dictum that a system cannot be considered scientific until it can be expressed in mathematical terms. It was not so difficult to forgive the plethora of confusing and sometimes seemingly contradictory signs in the *Elements* because behind it lay a model of the periodic table and the hope of a new order in chaos. In the present work no such hope sustains us in the face of the proliferation of mathematics-like notations, pseudo-equations, followed by arrows, dots, lines, arrows over (or should it be under?) words and not just Greek letters but Greek words. How are we to bear such an assault on our mentality? Is Bion Patient B in disguise? One could cite a hundred sentences that are at least as equivocal as the patient's 'girl who left about her knickers'.

Before we consign the book to the fire and regret the 25s net that it cost in 1965, let us consider another vertex, as he insists on calling point-of-view. What is this modern-day psychoanalytical Leonardo up to? What is Bion, the phenomenon, about? Let us say that in *Learning* he was trying to build a flying machine out of bits of apparatus called alpha-function on the model of the baby's illusion that it could fly to the breast and that he succeeded in getting a few feet off the ground for a few seconds. That few feet and few seconds was thrilling enough to suggest that he has succeeded in developing what might some day be the air-foil of learning theory. In the *Elements* he tried to make astrological table for predicting the evolution of the world of thought and succeeded at least in demonstrating that the cosmos of thought was composed of discrete bodies in ordered relation to one another, even if hopelessly complex for our feeble minds to grasp in its entirety or ever use for prediction. In *Transformations* he could be said to be working out the navigational instruments for steering his little flying machine amongst the stars once a suitable propulsive force could be devised. Let us see how far he succeeds from the vertex of this model. See how quickly one begins to talk Bionese, if not completely without tears.

What then does this model mean in less fanciful terms and how does it help us to understand his method of work and exposition? This would-be circumnavigator of the cosmos of thought seems to set about things in a rather child-like way which may in fact be the method that mathematicians use. It is suggested in his 'psychoanalytic game' with the Grid and his hope of 'mere manipulation of arbitrary symbols'. It is a game but a serious one and seems to go like this. First you must make a psychoanalytical observation. This is essential, and much of Chapter 3 (cf. pp. 29 and 47) is devoted to a detailed description of the requirements for so doing (one of his fireworks which must not, however, detain us at the moment). Next you collect your tools for calculation and apply them to the data of your observation. Finally you try to recognize how inadequate these tools are and set about modifying them to apply once again to the observation. The book conveys the impression that this series of events takes place at least three times, once through Chapters 1–5, for the second time in Chapters 6–9 and a third time in Chapters 10–12.

In that sense the book can be read as not so much an exposition of Bion's ultimate thought but as a record of his thinking and a document of his method of thought. For this reason it often gives the impression of being repetitive, inconsistent and wildly veering with changes in the intellectual wind. With this model in mind the plan of these three chapters devoted to *Transformations* will veer accordingly.

The first episode, Chapters 1–5, is built around three observations – patients A, B and C – representing instances of what Bion calls 'rigid motion' transformation (equivalent to Freud's original description of the transference), 'projective transformation' (related to Melanie Klein's concept of early transference based on part-objects, internal objects, splitting and projective identification) and a parasitic transference in which 'the patient draws on the love, benevolence and indulgence of the host' with the aim of destroying these same qualities. The equipment Bion uses to examine these observations is drawn mainly from *Learning* and *Elements* in addition to such established theories of the analytic method as countertransference. His business, as be stresses again and again, is not with psychoanalytical theories of the personality but with the theory of psychoanalytical observation of the personality. He is planning to develop what he hopefully calls 'the Theory of Transformations' as if it already existed sprung fully armed from his thigh. But we must not be misled; its structure is skeletal, consisting of three moves – O, T-alpha and T-beta (the 'facts', the experience of them, and the transformation of them which gives them a possibility of growth and accretion of meaning). The 'growth' involved is 'growth of mental formulation', A to H on the Grid, increase in complexity, sophistication and level of abstraction. This growth increases the generality of the mental formulation but thereby increases the specificity of the uses to which it can be put (horizontal axis). Behind this skeleton of equipment there lies a model, or rather two models. One is the model of the landscape painter transforming a scene of poppies in a field into pigment on canvas meant for public viewing. The second is the model of a lake reflecting trees disturbed by wind and a viewer seeing only the water. It is the same as Plato's image of the Cave but with the image disturbed, meaning disturbed by emotion, L, H and K.

Two things strike one immediately. First of all we hear nothing of psychoanalytical objects composed of sensa, myth and passion in this book. So the question must arise: is the theory of transformations a new attempt to formulate the objects of psychoanalytical observation and interpretation? The answer is almost certainly affirmative, though Bion makes no such reference. Second, we must wonder if Bion is tackling with his theory the same one essentially assaulted by Freud in the *Traumdeutung* as the problem of the dream work by which the latent dream-thought was converted into the manifest content of the dream image. Again the answer is almost certainly affirmative although again Bion makes no such link. Perhaps it is implied in his use of the idea of 'work' involved in 'growth' (p. 42). If so it would imply a great modification of Freud's idea which saw the work as employed to hide the truth from the dream censor rather than to give form to nascent thought. This latter would be Bion's view, despite his reservations about 'form' which seems so implicit in the very term 'transformation' (p. 12). Where he is in agreement with Freud is in relating thought and dream to a place midway between impulse and action, which he construes as essentially the capability to deal with problems of relations to objects in their absence. This view of dream and thought seems somehow to beg the question of Melanie Klein's view of the concreteness of internal objects which Bion appears to espouse. It seems at variance with his earlier work on the 'psychotic part of the personality' and the concept of bizarre objects.

In order to get to the heart of this first attempt at formulating the 'theory of transformations' it is necessary to quote at some length from Ch. 4:

> It is sometimes assumed that the motive for scientific work is an abstract love of the truth. The argument I have followed implies that the grounds for limiting the values that may be substituted for Ta-beta [analyses transformation] to true statements lies in the nature of values not so limited and their relationship to other components of the T [transformation] theory. If truth is not essential to all values of Ta-beta, Ta-beta must be regarded as expressed in and by manipulation of the emotions of patient or public' [what he has already called propaganda] 'and not in or by the interpretation; truth is essential for any value of Ta-beta in art or science. How is truth to be a criterion for a value proposed to Ta-beta? To what has it to be true and how shall we decide whether it is or not? Almost any answer appears to make truth contingent on some circumstance or idea that is contingent itself. Falling back on analytic experience for a clue, I am reminded that healthy mental growth seems to depend on truth as the living organism depends on food. If it is lacking or deficient the personality deteriorates. I cannot support this conviction by evidence regarded as scientific. It may be that the formulation belongs to the domain of Aesthetic. In practice the problem arises with schizoid personalities in whom the super-ego appears to be developmentally prior to the ego and to deny development and existence itself to the ego. The usurpation by the super-ego of the position that should be occupied by the ego involves imperfect development of the reality principle, exaltation of a "moral" outlook and lack of respect for the truth. The result is starvation of the psyche and stunted growth. I shall regard this statement as an axiom that resolves more difficulties than it creates'. (p. 37)

It will be recalled that in the previous chapter it was suggested that in restricting Ps↔D to the status of mechanism (disintegration-integration) rather than taking paranoid-schizoid and depressive positions in the ultimate sense of Mrs Klein's formulation as economic principles related to value attitude, Bion was creating more difficulties than he was resolving, to paraphrase him. It was also suggested that this paralleled his omission of a category of 'aesthetic' in the vertical 'growth' axis of the Grid. He appears now to be correcting both of these deficiencies, although it may appear that he is using the term 'value' only in a mathematical sense. But it leads on to a new exploration of the role of L, H and K in processes of thought and thus in analytic observation and interpretation. It can be seen that he has fairly promptly discovered that his skeletal navigational equipment is going to be inadequate for the cosmos he wishes to explore because that cosmos does not in fact correspond to his more astrological than astronomical table. But it also does not correspond, Bion recognizes, to Freud's model of the mind or of the psychoanalytical method. Where Freud was content to see his task as 'finite', namely in conducting transactions between realms of conscious and unconscious, Bion now realizes that he is traversing an infinite cosmos of meaning and only limiting himself to a 'finite universe of discourse' for the purpose of investigation and exposition. This is a major alteration in model of the method, one which is implicit in Melanie Klein's work with its forward, developmental orientation, as against Freud's essentially backward, reconstructive and psychopathological orientation. Hindsight always carries the deceptive implication that predictions could have been made if only the factors in the field had been adequately known. A forward view that sees the infinite possibilities despairs of such predictive power. Accordingly much of Chapter 5 is devoted by Bion to attacking the concept of causality in the realm of mental functions, a problem which Freud had skirted around by positing 'overdetermination' in place of determinism.

The upshot of this coming to terms with the infinite possibilities in mental function is that Bion must fall back on a more general position that the analyst's equipment is his personality in some state of partial analysis plus his training and experience in the use of the psychoanalytic method. This would seem to make nonsense of the idea of naive participation in the O of the treatment situation unless one realizes that by 'naive' he means not being empty, but rather being open. In terms of the Grid this means: 'Therefore the analyst's state of mind [i.e. in free-floating attention] should not be limited to categories E4 and F4 [conception plus attention and inquiry], say, but rather to the area of categories C to F by 1, 3, 4, 5 [myth, pre-conception, conception, concept plus definatory hypothesis, notation, attention and inquiry]' (p. 50). He thus must admit, in describing a clinical situation, 'When I thought I grasped his meaning it was often by virtue of an aesthetic rather than a scientific experience' (p. 52). He is moving away from the preoccupation with science as explanatory and towards an aesthetic conception of psychoanalytic thought (or Ta-beta) as the observation of phenomena and their meaningful organization to form the analyst's opinion of what is going on in the consulting room, and by extension, in the past and present lives of the two members present, analyst and patient. Only the tyrannical 'super'-ego (which probably means a tyrannical part of the self in projective identification with the superego) is interested to establish the cause of things in order to assign blame and prescribe punishment: 'The theory of causation is only valid in the domain of morality and only morality can cause anything. Meaning has no influence outside the psyche and causes nothing' (p. 59, note 1). Or further on: 'The group is dominated by morality – I include of course the negative sense that shows as rebellion against morality – and this contributes to the atmosphere of hostility to individual thought on which Freud remarked' (p. 64, note 2).

One might think that at this point the whole project is in ruins, that the possibility of precision has been destroyed by the prospect of the infinite possibilities of meaning, by the analyst being reduced to having a mere opinion of what is going on in the patient's mind and of mental events anyhow having no causal chain arrangement but being rather field and pattern problems, available only to aesthetic intuitions. The attempt to establish a theory of transformations to describe the methods of observation and communication in the consulting-room seems to have had the same abortive result as the conceptual experiment with psychoanalytical objects. But Bion seems to do one of his brilliant turnabouts and fetches back the idea of 'binocular vision' as the basis of reality testing and gives it a new meaning. Where in previous work (*Elements*) he had ascribed reality testing to the operation on the one hand of 'common sense' (that is, the correlation of the senses at the level of the emotional experience being observed and worked upon by alpha-function) and to the differentiation of conscious from unconscious effected by the 'membrane' of the 'contact-barrier' thrown up by alpha-function, he now proposes a new meaning, an addendum, to the idea of binocular vision. Perhaps it can be effected by transformations (alpha-function?) of the emotional experience from different points of view (vertices) which can be correlated. This seems to promise a possibility of understanding in greater detail the impact of the different emotional linkages, L. H and K that are operative in the transformation, in the creation of vessels of thought that can grow and accrete meaning, a new significance to the operation of 'love of the truth' to set against the intolerance to frustration, hatred of reality, attacks on linking, parasitism, etc. But it does seem to make some nonsense of his division between L and K and rather to suggest that they are really one, in the Keatsian sense 'Beauty is truth, truth beauty/ That is all ye know on earth and all ye need to know'.

> But the problem can also be regarded as concerned with the appropriateness of the grid as an instrument to be used for investigating L or H links. Considering the horizontal axis, there is no difficulty in retaining the headings found useful for K because an L relationship clearly cannot be regarded as excluding K either in logic or in reality. (p. 70)

So the second experiment in describing the analytic situation has collapsed by the end of Chapter 5 but already a new orientation has been achieved and the new equipment is at hand for the third onslaught.

CHAPTER TEN

Analytic truth and the operation of multiple vertices

I n the previous chapter it was suggested that *Transformations* could be read as a series of experiments in thought aimed at describing the method of psychoanalytical observation as serial transformations of observable 'facts' into thoughts capable of 'growth' and accretion of meaning, and further that this series of experiments can be visualized as conducted in a particular way. The method seems akin to that of the mathematician who invents arbitrary signs and rules for their manipulation and sees how far they carry him before new signs and rules need to be invented. The first such experiment, in the *Elements*, employed signs called psychoanalytical objects composed of three grid categories from the 'growth' axis, sensa (A), myth (C) and passion (row G, mysteriously). It seemed never to get off the ground (if we may return to the model of Leonardo's flying machine intended to navigate the cosmos of the mind). The second experiment (Chapters 1–5 of *Transformations*) employed simple navigational instruments called transformations but soon discovered that they were somehow produced by love of the truth and an aesthetic sense which was a function of the analyst's total personality plus training and experience, and anyhow resulted in nothing grander than his 'opinion' of what was happening in the consulting room.

So experiment three was initiated by remodelling the concept of 'binocular vision' originally outlined in *Learning* as a function of the correlation of the conscious and unconscious, delineated by the elaboration of the 'contact barrier' composed of the 'membrane' of alpha-elements. It was now to be remodelled in a way that might give some substance to the 'empty' differentiation of conscious–unconscious by filling them with differing points-of-view (now to be called 'vertices' in order to eliminate the bias in favour of visual criteria suggested by 'viewpoint'). Chapter 6 introduces the new experiment. By remodelling the problem of psychoanalytical communication through employing 'love of the truth' (K link), the question of the present and absent object comes to the fore. Pain and tension which favours hatred of the truth (minus-K link) becomes the stimulus as well as the deterrent of thought, seen now as essentially a technique for solving problems about objects in their absence. Bion illustrates the way in which the mind may employ different sensuous vertices, say sight, smell and hearing, by analogy with the way in which the mathematician may deal with the relation of point, line and circle by pre-Cartesian, Cartesian and algebraic means. He is incidentally interested in suggesting that such mathematical problems and their solutions have psychic reality, but this rather adds confusion to the exposition and need not detain us here.

The prototype problem Bion utilizes is the disappearance of the breast, leaving only a point where it used to be, in a field where it may have disappeared either outside or inside the mind (circle). He suggests that a precondition for the solution of this problem, i.e. to be able to think about the breast in its absence or when it has been replaced by the presence of a no-breast (point), is the capacity to bear the pain of the possibility that this observed phenomenon is meaningless. This might be felt as intolerable because the breast, as the container of all meaning, might be felt as destroyed if meaninglessness were acknowledged as a possibility: 'Since the first requisite for the discovery of the meaning of any conjunction depends on the ability to admit that the phenomena may have no meaning, an inability to admit that they may have no meaning stifles the possibility of curiosity at the outset' (p. 81).

This prototype can be applied just as well to problems of time and problems of space as to substantive objects, and thus would have application to psychopathological manifestations such as megalomania and depersonalization as well as hallucination.

So this third experiment in describing psychoanalytical observation, thought and communication in terms of the means by which observation is transformed into thought which can grow in complexity, sophistication and level of abstraction, and in doing so accrete meaning, has been narrowed down to experiences of absent objects and tolerance to the pain of acknowledging their continued existence, this being contingent on the ability to be curious about the meaning of the phenomenon by acknowledging that it might be without meaning. The ability to think depends on reality testing through 'binocular vision', where the two 'views' are different vertices in the sense of different fields or orderings of the world, say different sense modalities, or other 'positions'. These other positions seem to include models or myths or metaphors, which also include the senses, as in an alimentary or respiratory model of relationship to the world. Vertices of 'sense' and 'system' may also be extended by vertices of 'position', perhaps in the meaning of value attitudes as in Mrs Klein's use of the term. Bion even speaks of the vertex of the 'reproductory system', but does not succeed in making clear if this is the same as 'from the point-of-view of sex' as he had used this in the *Elements*.

It is curious, considering the idea of multiple vertices, that Bion perseveres in considering verbalization as essential for thought to 'grow' in sophistication beyond the realm of dream and myth (row C), as if he could conceive no notational system other than language. Perhaps he means 'language' and 'verbal' in a very broad sense, but it seems strongly suggested that the problems of external communication ('publication') become confused with thought as internal communication. This may be seen in Bion's discussion of the need for 'rules' of transformation. Perhaps some of the difficulty lies in his employment of the artist's activity as the model for transformations, a difficulty not inherent in the model of the reflection of trees in the water disturbed by wind, which makes a link both with Plato's image of the cave and Wittgenstein's concept of 'seeing as'.

Although there can be no doubt of Bion's commitment to meaning as an inner-world phenomenon which borrows forms from the external world to construct its dream-narratives, he is less unequivocal about the concreteness of this inner world: 'If there is a no-thing, the thing must exist. By analogy, if Falstaff is a no-thing Falstaff also exists: if it can be said that Falstaff, Shakespeare's character who had no real existence, has more "reality" than people who existed in fact, it is because an actual Falstaff exists: the invariant under psychoanalysis is the ratio of no-thing to thing' (p. 103). The operative phrase seems to be 'if it can be said' which seems to confuse the problem of the limits of language with that of the limits of thought. From the viewpoint of psychoanalytical concepts as tools, this confuses the problem of what can be thought about with what exists in psychic reality: objects of imagination confused with internal objects. This seems a surprising bind for Bion to get into when he had already specified that the problems of meaning deal with an infinite, not a finite universe: that is, that anything can be thought, as mathematics marvellously illustrates: ordinal numbers, imaginary numbers, the square root of minus 2, etc.

So it seems suggested that at this point Bion's third experiment is beginning to crumble because of his confusing the absent object or no-thing with an internal object or no-thing. Correspondingly the construction which he puts upon 'non-existent' objects and the paradox of the patient who is identified with such an object, is approached by way of the stripping of meaning rather than the construction of the bizarre object. Thus one can begin to see how the search for evolution of thought by way of the Grid is leading him further and further from the concreteness of psychic reality expressed in his earliest formulation of bizarre objects as formed by agglomeration of minutely fragmented objects. Under the Grid the formation of a delusional system could be 'nowhere' and in 'no time' but it could not be 'a world in which he could live', as Freud said of Schreber's system. 'The domain of thought may be conceived of as a space occupied by no-things; the space occupied by a particular no-thing is marked by a sign such as the words "chair" or "cat"' (p. 106). By this restriction he imposes upon himself another restriction: 'by thought I mean, in this context, that which enables problems to be solved in the absence of the object' (p. 107). A tautology. He continues: 'Indeed unless the object is absent there is no problem.' But this dictum is then begged: 'The problem is associated with the sense that the realization only approximates to the pre-conception.' This implies that the only problems in life are those of dis-satisfaction. But he has already spoken of the developmental difficulties that can arise through a too-understanding object, corresponding to Melanie Klein's view that an optimal level of anxiety was needed for development to be forwarded.

The blind alley into which he has got himself through his adamant refusal to be 'deterred from discussing a point merely because it is inconceivable', results in an interesting evocation of the biological concept of 'tropism' into the realm of the mind by postulating a consciousness attached to beta-elements as 'an awareness of a lack of existence that demands an existence, a thought in search of a meaning'. This is after all like a pre--conception which he has already assumed by definition to be unobservable. This is Bion at his most recalcitrant, unable to read his own notes but still claiming to be able to use them for contrasting with one another (p. 109). But he is always amusing when he realizes he is in trouble: 'The argument is, I think, circular: I am relying on the adequacy of the circle's diameter' (p. 111). This could hardly mean anything but that the spurious origins of the argument will have been lost sight of by the time its conclusions are reached.

What does finally emerge quite clearly from this investigation of the denudation of meaning, minus K, retrograde movement in the Grid, return to beta-elements by alpha-process working backwards (to mention the various forms in which the problem has been stated at various places in these three books) is a new formulation in terms of vertices, which are now called 'positions', because the image is of points on a circle with arrows pointing in or out. A footnote acknowledges that this formulation of the vertex or position of minus K stands in relation to Melanie Klein's concept of the paranoid-schizoid positions as 'two views of a reversible perspective'. This point is then further illustrated by clinical reference to claustrophobia and agoraphobia to show how the 'unsophisticated' and 'intuitive' psychoanalytical formulation can be reconciled with a 'sophisticated' and 'precise geometric' formulation. This is meant to serve both as an illustration of binocular vision from differing vertices and as an example of the direction in which Bion feels formulation of psychological problems needs to move in order to create a notation that will serve equally well for all the fields that deal with the activities of the mind such as the arts, and presumably social sciences, history, philosophy, etc. None of it is convincing but Bion never means to be, only thought provoking.

What thought, then, has this middle section, this so-called third experiment in formulating the transactions of psychoanalysis, and thus of observation and thought, provoked? Bion, on the background of the formulations in *Learning* and *Elements* has investigated observation and thought on the basis of the relationship between the representation of present and absent objects in the mind; using the breast again as prototype object, but widening his scope to consider also time and space as objects, existence and non-existence as dimensions, meaningful and meaningless as possibilities, and the geometry of point and line as his method of inquiry and exposition. In this widened theatre love of the truth and hatred of the truth (linked to intolerance of mental pain, envy and destructiveness), have been represented to operate, with reference to the Grid, in opposite directions with respect to growth and accretion of meaning. The upshot has been a rapprochement with the Kleinian theories of positions as value systems and also with the concept of psychic reality as related to the concrete conception of mental spaces. But Bion has run into difficulty over the question of the existence of absent objects, the no-things that can be represented by point and line with reference to the spaces that can be represented by inside and outside the circle. His geometrical system of representations, will not make certain distinctions, such as between imagined objects of thought and internal objects which exist inside and can be expelled from the mental space. It will also not make an adequate distinction between the objects and spaces of psychic reality and the unreal objects (bizarre objects) that have their non-existence in the no-where of the delusional system. He has further had to beg the question of the nature of the absence of absent objects. But the experiment is far from a total loss. On the gain side we can say with confidence that the concept of vertices has broadened the flexibility of the idea of positions. It gives a new scope for developing the conception of the 'world' in which a person is living at a particular moment, and opens the way to a new view of splitting processes. Bion has given us in this section a method for conceptualizing the nature of the different parts of the self, not only in terms of psychic tendencies (Melanie Klein) but in terms of the different worlds that each may inhabit, where 'world' is the object of 'vertex'. He has laid the basis for the systematic consideration of dimensionality, and the work in this direction embodied in *Explorations in Autism* [Meltzer et al, 1975] can be viewed as one of its fruits. While he seems to dream of a notation, at once precise and sophisticated, his real contribution seems always to go in the opposite direction, of opening the door to new regions of phenomena which pose even greater problems for our feeble notation, built as it is, necessarily, on the primarily visual and deceptively narrative and pseudo-causal language of the dream. But he has helped us here by slaying the dragon of causality and opening the cosmos of the mind in its infinitude of possibility for the generating of meaning.

CHAPTER ELEVEN

'Learning about' as a resistance to 'becoming'

In the two previous chapters it was suggested that *Transformations* could be read as a series of experiments in mathematical modes of thought, beginning with the last part of *Elements* and continuing into *Attention and Interpretation*, aimed at evolving a language of precision for describing the methods of observation, thought and communication employed in the psychoanalytical method. The stimulus for this effort, starting with *Learning*, had been the recognition of the role played by disorders of thought in severe mental disturbance, (schizophrenia in particular), related also to phenomena described earlier as peculiar to basic assumption groups. What began as an attempt to avoid the 'penumbra of existing meaning' in ordinary words for the sake of positing an 'empty' hypothetical apparatus of thought: alpha-function, in *Learning*, expanded into a 'periodic table' of the 'elements' of thought, the Grid, from which Bion first attempted a description of 'psychoanalytical objects', tripartite 'molecules' compounded of sensa, myth and passion.

This first attempt seemed not to lead anywhere and a new attempt, an illustration of the 'psychoanalytic game', has been undertaken in *Transformations* using the Grid to trace the 'growth' of ideas. The second attempt, in the form of a 'theory of transformations' failed also but brought forward certain important realizations, such as the central role of aesthetic intuition, its relation to love of the truth, the slaying of the concept of causality in favour of exploration of an infinite universe of meaningful discourse, finally the humbling of the analyst to the position of merely offering 'opinion'. But a third attempt utilized a broadened idea of 'binocular vision' to erect a concept of multiplicity of vertices, again using a mathematizing format but more for analogic illustration than as an experimental method. The attempt to solve the problem seems to come to grief over the failure to distinguish between the internal world of L and K and the delusional world of H and minus K, but it does establish a basis for differential value systems, with special reference to thought and feeling about absent objects.

The fourth attempt to formulate a precise notation for psychoanalytical observation, thought and communication starts, therefore, on a fairly firm ground of K and minus K in dubious battle: the duel of angels, thought and feeling versus anti-thought and anti-feeling. The exposition in these last three chapters becomes gradually less mathematical, finally frankly Dodgsonian, and more theological in format. The initial model of the marbles on the tray as an analogue for the patient's statements-on-the-grid, as it were, brings forward again the inconsistency in the structure of the Grid. Is minus K to be represented by column 2, or by retrograde movement (anti-growth) on the Grid or by a mirror image, an anti-grid? Bion seems to compromise in his elucidation of 'transformation in hallucinosis': 'Transformation, in rigid motion or in projection, must be seen to have hallucinosis as one of its media' (p. 131). The brilliant investigation of the 'milkman cometh' material seems to suggest that hallucinosis belongs to the realm of delusion formation and that its phenomenology would better be encompassed by an anti-grid. This would differentiate such a process from retrograde movement on the grid as the realm of minus K and justify (p. 129) 'the assumption underlying loyalty to the K link (which) is that the personality of analyst and analysand can survive the loss of its protective coating of lies, subterfuge, evasion and hallucination and may even be fortified and enriched by the loss'. The suggestion of an antigrid would remove 'hallucination' from this list and have implications for what was earlier (and will be again later) called 'catastrophic change' and is soon to be called 'transformation in O'.

For reasons that become clearer in *Attention,* Bion seems keen to establish the category of the mystic who claims to be able to make contact with the 'ultimate reality' of Platonic forms, or godhead or Kantian thing-in-itself. This seems unfortunate at this point and rather confuses the issue of the discussion, particularly as this ultimate reality is outside the operation of good and evil, of K and minus K, of reality versus delusion. It gives a mystical fogginess to the exposition of mysterious processes of growth and seems unnecessary since in *Learning* Bion had already made a sufficient distinction between 'learning from experience' which changes the learner and 'learning about' which only adds to his stock of information. One can see that it is necessary for the investigation of megalomania, and for the way in which the patient's megalomania taxes the analyst's capacity to distinguish between love for the truth and megalomania in himself. But the whole discussion of hallucinosis, megalomania, 'hyperbole' in the expression of emotion and the distinction between 'acts' and 'acting out' detracts from the investigation of resistance as an analytic phenomenon because it does not allow for a differentiation of the motive for resistance. Bion is finally driven to acknowledge this distinction, resistance to mental pain and resistance arising out of the nature of the individual; but the opportunity for clarity is already lost. Nonetheless, Chapter 10 is a splendid elucidation of the problem of the megalomanic and deluded character and the special difficulties of the analyst in coping with him:

> The impression such patients give of suffering from a character disorder derives from the sense that their wellbeing and vitality spring from the same characteristics that give trouble. The sense that loss of the bad parts of his personality is inseparable from loss of that part in which all his mental health resides, contributes to the acuity of the patient's fears. (p. 144)

Accordingly Chapters 11 and 12 can be read as Bion's last flirtation with mathematical formulation: 'Transformation in K has, contrary to the common view, been less adequately expressed by mathematical formulation than by religious formulations' (p. 156). From this point on, having consigned his own mathematics to the Dodgsonian or Alice-in-Wonderland category with wry humour, his thought will move onto the more religious plane, in keeping with the theory of internal objects:

> The gap between reality and the personality or, as I prefer to call it, the inaccessibility of O, is an aspect of life with which analysts are familiar under the guise of resistance. Resistance is only manifest when the threat is contact with what is believed to be real. There is no resistance to anything because it is believed to be false. Resistance operates because it is feared that the reality of the object is imminent. (p. 147)

Thus the question concerning the psychoanalytic process, and particularly the part in it played by interpretation, can be resolved by Bion into the following formulation: 'Is it possible through psychoanalytic interpretation to effect a transition from knowing the phenomena of the real self to being the real self' (p. 148). This is his way of stating the problem of the integration of split-off parts as one of the dimensions of growth of the personality. It also brings him up against the problem of whether good and evil are necessary categories of the personality's vertices, a problem suggested, after all, by Melanie Klein's intuition that splitting-and-idealization was the first move in personality development. In Bion's language such a move would not constitute a realization of a pre-conception but rather the use of a conception as a pre-conception (cycle 2).

Essentially Bion seems to fall back on the fear of the unknown, the intolerance of uncertainty, its connection with impotence, awe, dependence, responsibility in the face of ignorance. These he finds are the ultimate factors militating against perseverance in the search for the truth. It is not clear whether he considers the use of number for the sake of 'binding' constant conjunctions and a preliminary step in 'winning from the void and formless infinite' as a step in K or in minus K in this 'Alice' world, but one is reminded of the constant conjunction of numerology with mystical systems for explaining the universe. Clearly he has little use for quantitative statements in the realm of interpretation. The crux of the matter of interpretation seems to find the following expression: 'The interpretation should be such that the transition from knowing about reality to becoming real is furthered. This transition depends on matching the analysand's statement with an interpretation which is such that the circular argument remains circular but has an adequate diameter' (p. 153). This takes us back to what seemed a bit of Puckish intransigence in an earlier chapter and is now to be made absolutely central. What does Bion mean? The statement which follows is either arrant nonsense or mystically profound. Let us assume the former, since it makes it possible to examine the situation, while the cloud of new terminology of orbits, complementarity, etc, can only stop the conversation. Let us assume that Bion is shamelessly trying to maintain that a circular argument can go somewhere other than up its own tail, and is prepared to shoot off his numerological fireworks to blind us to this obscurantism. Why should he do this?

If we follow the Bionic logic we would have to say that he is illustrating minus K, column 2, creation of beta-screens, etc, in the service of hiding from himself and the reader that he is in trouble. His further recourse to identification with Newton as mathematical genius and theological zany (or 'gaga' in Keynes's terms) does not reassure. The fact seems to be that he is in trouble and Bion in trouble, like Freud in trouble, is often at his most dazzlingly wordy and erudite. The trouble seems to centre on Bion's preoccupation with the function of interpretations and the question of their 'acceptance' by the patient, whether in the service of K or minus K, whether in K or in O: 'Any interpretation may be accepted in K but rejected in O; acceptance in O means that acceptance of an interpretation enabling a patient to "know" that part of himself to which attention has been drawn is felt to involve "being" or "becoming" that person' (p. 164). The price to be paid may, Bion thinks, be excessive when felt as involving madness, murder, megalomania, etc. Again a brilliant clinical formulation is brought for exemplification but the case is too special to substantiate the general conclusions Bion is trying to reach. In this way he seems to get quite far away from the experience of the transference as the therapeutic process and to return to earlier formulations of Freud regarding transference resistances, development of insight and working through. Consequently he tends to present a picture of the analyst as wielding powerful intellectual equipment for making instantaneous decisions based on precise judgments at a very high level of sophistication and abstraction. Bion of course knows very well that such a picture is ludicrous when confronted with the mediocrity of practising analysts:

> Epistemologically a statement may be regarded as evolved when any dimension can have a grid category assigned to it. For purpose of interpretation the statement is insufficiently evolved until its column 2 dimension is apparent. When the column 2 dimension has evolved, the statement can be said to be ripe for interpretation; its development as material for interpretation has reached maturity. (p. 167)

This sounds distressingly like many of the old dicta for timing of interpretation but in fact probably says nothing very much more than that the defensive function of the patient's material needs to be recognized before any proper interpretation, i.e. a meta-psychological statement regarding the transference, can possibly be made. It seems reasonable to suggest that the whole section about circular arguing and the need for the correct diameter to the circle is a bit of the old Dodgsonian leg-pull, behind which is a really serious observation and suggestion: 'the conditions [for interpretation] are complete when the analyst feels aware of resistance in himself – not countertransference – but resistance to the response he anticipates from the analysand if he gives the interpretation' (p. 168). In other words if it does not take courage to say, it probably is not the truth of what you think of the patient's material. The courage required relates to the potential explosiveness of the truth, which may certainly, as Bion asserts again and again, be the food of the mind but also threatens the person, really analyst and patient alike, with the catastrophic change of becoming a different person. This thesis is rather beautifully illustrated in the hypothetical 'sun will rise tomorrow' example, where it can be seen that courage is required to expose the hostility and paranoia that lie behind idealizations.

So the book ends on a rather wry note which implies a somewhat sad farewell to a dream of precise formulation, psychoanalytic games, rules for the practice of psychoanalysis: 'The transition from sensibility to awareness, of a kind suitable to be the foundation of action, cannot take place unless the process of change, T-alpha, is mathematical though perhaps in a form that has not been recognized as such' (p. 171). This seems really to mean, stripped of its wiliness: if you want to act rather than think, use quantitative modes of thought but do not let yourself know you are doing it. One cannot disrespect the quality of thought and erudition that Bion has mustered for his flirtation with precision, but the whole structure, from *Learning* through *Transformations* could be dismissed as 'gaga' were it not for the constantly fruitful penetration of the psychoanalytical method which nestles somehow amidst the mathematizing, or more correctly runs like a seam of ore through the granite of wilful manipulation of arbitrary signs and rules. What remains, when the scaffolding is removed, that some people find a work of genius in these three books, taken together as the prelude to *Attention and Interpretation*?

It could be cogently suggested that by the end of *Transformations* the art of psychoanalysis and the science of psychoanalysis have been welded together and placed on a foundation no longer isolated from the other fields that deal with human mentality – psychology, sociology, history, philosophy, theology, the fine arts, anthropology, palaeontology. This foundation is method, and Bion has done what Freud with his 'pure gold' scorned to do and Melanie Klein was not equipped to do. All these books, despite their clinical stimulation by phenomena met in the consulting room in the therapy of schizophrenia, thought disorders, etc., are really examinations of the psychoanalytical method. It has been said that the poet is always writing about poetry and the painter is always investigating painting. Bion can be said to be making a systematic attempt to discover what psychoanalysis is about, not from the point of view of its objects of study but rather from the experience of the analyst. He is therefore, as he reminds us, not evolving psychoanalytic theories (these he assures us are well cared for by the scientific committee of the psychoanalytical societies) but theories about psychoanalysis as a thing-in-itself.

In order to justify such a sweeping statement, it is necessary to attempt a summary of the structure of thought which does in fact emerge when the mathematical scaffolding is removed, as it has in fact been somewhat stripped in the foregoing chapters. This is needed also as a baseline in order to appreciate the magnitude of the undertaking and achievement in *Attention*. Perhaps it could be reasonably stated as follows:

The realm of the mind is a world of infinite possibilities of meaning from whose formlessness a coherent internal world must be constructed by thought operating on the perception of emotional experiences. An apparatus, mysteriously modelled on the mother's capacity for reverie, is developed in infancy for the purpose of deriving from these experiences thoughts which may be used for thinking. But at the same time a rival organization for creating lies which can only be used for creating delusions and bizarre objects, or else for evacuation, is developed, the former nourishing the mind for growth, the latter poisoning it. Psychoanalysis is a method for studying the interaction of these two organizations through the medium of the transference and countertransference, which can reveal the methods by which the mental pain involved in facing the truth is either modified or evaded, mainly through attacks on the linking which the growth of thought creates. This growth, which proceeds in sophistica-tion, complexity and level of abstraction by being put to different uses, depends on the operation, either internally or with an exter-nal object, by which the disordered and painful thought finds a container that can modify it by means of a shift in value system, or vertex, or view-of-the world. These painful thoughts are in essence concerned with the meaning of the absence of objects of love and dependence, for without them the self is overwhelmed with despair and nameless dread. But the problem of distinguish-ing between the evasion of pain and its modification requires reality testing, which in essence is the differentiation between truth and lies, understanding and mis-understanding. This is done by correlating the understanding derived from more than one vertex as well as by using the new thought as a pre-conception whose realization may be evaluated for its degree of approxima-tion to expectation. In assisting the patient to improve his mental functions and grow in his mental structure the analyst is reduced to offering his opinion, often based more on intuitive aesthetic judgments than precise intellectual evaluation. This latter can, however, be supplemented in tranquil recollection.

CHAPTER TWELVE

The bondage of memory and desire

An approach to *Attention and Interpretation* is probably only possible for someone already 'hardened' to Bion's extraordinary demands upon the reader, for he goes his way in this book not only in the expectation that no one 'but a practising psychoanalyst can understand this book although I have done my best to make it simple' but that the reader will have not merely read but mastered the previous books, the Grid and the other quasi-mathematical paraphernalia. It is a book in which one of the two terms in the title hardly ever appears in the text. And yet attention is the underlying theme of the work.

Insofar as this book represents Bion's most organized attempt to present a theory of psychoanalytical practice, it tends to read a bit like a handbook for pilgrims to a strange world. Until they actually arrive and begin to have the experiences and encounter the objects described, it is all meaningless. The practising psychoanalyst who, Bion hopes, will be his reader may have practised analysis for many years without ever entering the world of Bion's description. This is not merely because he may not have treated schizophrenics, say, but rather that his 'vertex' has been so different. He may be sophisticated enough to have realized that the medical model was too crude for application to this method and consequently have taken to referring to his 'analysands' rather than his 'patients'. Readings in linguistic philosophy and philosophy of mind may have made him aware of the great difficulties inherent in the use of language for communication. His personal analysis may have humbled him to a state of tentativeness about his capacities to observe and understand himself and others. His study of the psychoanalytical literature may have warned him of the confusion and inadequacy of theoretical formulation in the field. Study of history may have enabled him to see or suspect that psychoanalysis had its historic roots more in philosophy and theology than in 19th-century science. But it is unlikely that any of this will have prepared him for the massive onslaught against his system of intellectual security that Bion's book represents.

In the earlier works the battering mainly took the form of feeling crushed by a sense of inferior intelligence as this massive equipment of language, signs and symbols was set into the field. Clearly one's intellectual house had been built of twigs at best and the Bion wolf was at the door. But actually it seemed all right; alpha-process did not hurt, the Grid turned out to be quite harmless, container and contained seemed almost familiar. One even began to feel a bit of a wolf that could huff and puff at other people's twiggy conceptions. So if one could bear the exasperation and persevere despite the bruising to one's vanity the outcome was quite pleasant. No, one had not taken to playing psychoanalytical games with the Grid in the evening instead of watching television nor had one's comprehension and interpretation of one's patients' material altered noticeably. The inner feeling of being different could not be substantiated from observation of feelings or behaviour, yet one knew that there was no choice; one was either with him, Bionic, or against him, minus Bionic. His thought had to be reckoned with.

But towards the end of *Transformations* the shift in vertex and language from the mathematical to the religious began to take place. Here in *Attention* a new and more difficult demand is being made upon the reader. He is being asked to throw away the work of two centuries, no, five centuries, of liberating the human mind from the bondage of religion and mysticism. The

Renaissance, the Reformation, the Age of Reason, the triumphs of the Scientific Method – all this we are being asked to jettison. Our carefully trained memories, our better-than-Christian desire to help our suffering fellows, our disciplined capacity for understanding – all this is bondage to the realm of the sensuous. We will never be able to enjoy hallucinations and thereby understand the patient who enjoys transformations in hallucinosis if we cling to the paltry sensuous world. By artificially blinding ourselves we can become able to pierce the light with a beam of darkness and un-see the un-real world of nothings.

That is meant to be Cycle 1, an illustration of the resistance to Bion's demands upon us by means of mockery. Cycle 2 could be said to be the rubbery technique, rolling-with-the-punch. 'But Bion isn't really saying anything different from what Freud said. It doesn't involve doing anything different from what I always do. I never keep notes any longer because I realize that my unconscious recollection and ordering of the patient's material is so much more profound than my conscious efforts. I long ago abandoned any desire to cure my patients because I saw clearly that the psychoanalytical method only reorganized the patient's defences and strengthened his hold on reality. Likewise the corrective emotional experience, which is the essence of the method, depends more on the realities of the analyst's personality than on his intellectual understanding, as Freud thought. I notice as does Bion that I fall asleep occasionally and wake with a rather painful sensation, but this is due to deep contact with my patient's unconscious. In the final reckoning those patients who are able to develop faith in the truth and goodness of the analytical method and their particular analyst thrive and those who cannot leave. So I am basically in agreement with Wilfred but find his way of writing a bit tiresome.'

Cycle 3, the heretic hunter of the Scientific Establishment: 'Under the guise of scientific rigour and linguistic precision Bion is clearly trying to wreck an edifice of theory and technique which has been built by devoted workers over the better part of a century. In Bion's early work, with which I feel in deep sympathy, he was setting about making a rapprochement between mathematical modes of thought and the psychoanalytical theory of the personality as a teachable discipline that could strengthen the student against being swept into action by the countertransference evoked by very disturbed patients. This was extremely useful potentially, had he succeeded, because it is well recognized that the training analysis of our very carefully selected candidates does not give them a comparable experience on the couch while, on the other hand, it is also recognized that more and more our consulting rooms are filled with borderline patients as the liberalizing of sexual morality, brought about by psychoanalysis, has greatly diminished the prevalence of the neuroses for whose treatment the method was designed. It was disturbing in the earlier works to see references to 'the infinite', Meister Eckhart and the 'religious vertex', but he now seems to have abandoned himself quite completely to an idealization of confusion. He is, after all, rather old now and his so-called novel, *A Memoir of the Future* is quite absurd and I do not mean in the Kierkegaardian sense, though it has a resemblance to that madman' s ravings.'

Having thus set aside these three bits of ourselves – the mocker, the rubberman and the future president of the society – we can set about trying to understand what Bion means and how it is an outgrowth of the earlier work, not an abandonment of it, even though the vertex and the paraphernalia is rather changed. What really are the demands being made upon us? Let us do some reviewing. Freud's discovery of the role of the unconscious in the formation of certain mental aberrations produced the topographic model of the mind in which the original dreamlike world of hallucinatory wish-fulfilment under the sway of the pleasure principle was gradually relegated to sleep and the unconscious, while consciousness apprehended and acquiesced in a world of reality. Traumatic and unassimilated experiences of the infantile past continued to exert a pressure in dream-life and symptom formation. This was transformed in the 1920s into the structural model of the mind in which an ego, evolved from the id under the impact of reality learned to use anxiety as a signal in its service to three masters: the demands of the id, the impact of reality, and an internalization of parental authority – the super-ego. Conflict was aggravated by the operation in the id of contrary instincts of life and death. This model was changed by Melanie Klein to include a geography of phantasy in which the self occupied two worlds, internal and external, with which it carried on a continual commerce in meaning through processes of introjection and projection, gradually integrating itself and its objects from an earlier state, characterized by splitting and persecution, by the agency of good experiences and a depressive orientation.

Under Freud's model of the mind, both early and late, the psychoanalytical method was essentially a reconstructive one, whereby early experiences could be understood and the pain accepted and 'worked through' so that symptoms and character distortions could be given up. Under Melanie Klein's model psychoanalysis was essentially a method dependent on the evocation of the transference within which the infantile relationships to internal objects could be worked through from a state of splitting and persecution to one of integration and depressive orientation by means of insights contained in the analyst's interpretations. Under both of these models the great tool was observation of the transference, as resistance in Freud's model, as psychic reality in Klein's. In both the countertransference was the great hindrance and limitation. In both models emotional relationships and mental pain were the focus of attention.

Bion has been constructing an amplified model of the mind and an amplified model of the method of analysis. In Freud's model growth was taken for granted. In Melanie Klein's model the configuration, if not the achievement, of growth was taken for granted. In Bion's model growth is determined in its possibility and form only by virtue of a set of inherent pre-conceptions which require emotional experiences sufficiently congruent to serve as realizations in order that a system of conceptions may become gradually organized into concepts and a deductive system for experiencing the world. This is accomplished by alpha-function operating on the emotional experience and creating dream-thoughts which can be used for thinking so that, by the operation of container and contained, under the sway of movement back and forth between persecutory and depressive values (Ps↔D), these dream thoughts may grow in complexity, sophistication and abstractness into a scientific deductive system under the dominance of love of the truth and aesthetic intuition. The mythic dream-thought version of this scientific deductive system is represented by Melanie Klein's conception of the concreteness of psychic reality.

The amplified model of the psychoanalytical method that grows out of this amplified model of the mind has been under investigation in parallel with the elaboration of the model through *Elements* and *Transformations* with very little success, unless one strips off the scaffolding which was still needed to sustain its credibility. This scaffolding, quasi-mathematical logic and language, is now being sloughed and what comes under scrutiny first is the requirements of the analyst's state of mind in his consulting room so that he may function in a procedure that could be viewed as consonant with, possibly even conducive to, growth in both analysand and analyst. This state is said to be characterized by the eschewing of memory, desire and understanding. Bion is at great pains to explain what he means, but does so by introducing a new sign, F, which gathers such vague and confusing qualities that the outcome is rather despair-provoking. The reader cannot fail to sympathize at one point: 'The disciplined increase of F by suppression of K, or subordination of transformations in K to Transformations in O, is therefore felt as a very serious attack on the ego until F has become established' (p. 48). Why 'F'? Is it row F, 'concept'? He calls it an 'element'. It seems on the other hand to be F as in Freud to designate the attitude expressed by Freud in his letter to Lou Salomé where he spoke of 'artificially blinding myself'. Or is it F as in 'Frightful Fiend' of the Coleridge poem? Or is it F as in 'Act of Faith'? 'The "act of faith" (F) depends on disciplined denial of memory and desire. A bad memory is not enough: what is ordinarily called forgetting is as bad as remembering. It is necessary to inhibit dwelling on memories and desires' (p. 41).

Probably the most useful understanding is to take F as a compound of all of these: faith, fiend, Freud's blinding, and row F (concept) as a vertex which can produce the beam of darkness, the state of Keatsian negative capability, which can serve as a tool to investigate the utterly non-sensual world of psychic reality. This is Dante following Virgil. It is the feat that Orpheus and Lot's wife did not manage. But how does it differ from 'free-floating attention'? Or is it merely a more detailed description, or prescription for the achievement of, that vague but cherished state of mind? How does Bion's idea of faith harmonize with his idea that the foundations of curiosity lay in the capacity to admit the possibility of meaninglessness?

The idea of free-floating attention seems to be a simple one, conceived as simple to accomplish, on the model of free-floating in water, which does not require an act of faith in the buoyancy of the human body but merely a realization of it for a moment. The child may be required to exercise an act of faith in letting go of daddy or trying to swim without his water-wings, but that is based on experience of daddy's good will already in hand. Bion's act-of-faith would correspond more to floating free in shark-infested waters. It assumes that everyone has a fiend following him, is on the verge of hallucinosis, megalomania, delusions, catastrophic anxiety. There seems every reason to believe this, judging from the impact of drugs, isolation, group pressure, fever, etc. The question must arise, is it really possible to do such a thing in the cosy familiarity of one's own consulting-room, living in a fairly democratic country, with a nice spouse, money in the bank, no evidence of cancer, and a patient who has been paying his bill and coming regularly for years? Probably the answer is that it is not possible to achieve this state by practis-ing the discipline that Bion advocates because the 'suspension' of these functions is not possible by an act of the will. But it may be something that does, or might, happen in time with experience of practising the method of psychoanalysis. The act-of-faith would not be an act but a gradual transformation of the person into a psychoanalyst, if one takes this term to mean someone who believes that psychoanalysis exists, that it is a thing-in-itself. In any event Bion seems to suggest that this belief is contingent on the realization of the fiend in one's own mind, that hallucinosis, megalomania, delusion exist and are merely held at bay by some means. Melanie Klein would say they are held at bay by living in the sphere of good objects. Orwell would say the same, or conversely, by not living in the sphere of Big Brother. Evidence in the book suggests that for Bion the sharks that infest his waters are lawyers and judges hearing accusations against him of malpractice when he cannot defend himself, for he has forgotten his patient's name, doesn't even know if he is married and cannot deny that he fell asleep on various occasions in the consulting-room. A Kafkaesque world!

Suppose then that we accept that what Bion recommends may in fact happen in time to the practising psychoanalyst, how is it to be distinguished from deterioration? 'There are real dangers associated with the appearance (that the state of suspended memory and desire has to that of the severely regressed patient); this is why the procedure here adumbrated is advocated only for the psychoanalyst whose own analysis has been carried at least far enough for the recognition of paranoid-schizoid and depressive positions' (p. 47, footnote). But he must surely mean 'far enough for him to have had a glimpse of the frightful fiend in himself'. This would mean that he has at least come to distinguish that his most catastrophic anxieties relate not to death but to madness, to being devoured into insanity by a shark in himself.

What justification can Bion give for such an aspiration, whether it is to be achieved by his discipline or by the evolution of the person practising psychoanalysis? Is it necessary or is it only desirable in relation to a research interest in psychosis? Bion has several answers to this: 'I am concerned with developing a mode of thought which is such that a correct clinical observation can be made, for if that is achieved there is always hope of the evolution of the appropriate theory' (p. 44). In other words any correct clinical observation is impaired by the operation of memory and desire. Second, he seems to believe that the unimpeded evolution of the transference requires this state in the analyst: 'If the analyst has not deliberately divested himself of memory and desire the patient can "feel" this and is dominated by the "feeling" that he is possessed by and contained in the analyst's state of mind, namely, the state represented by the term "desire"' (p. 42). Third, he believes that the problem of envy in the transference is very much aggravated by the analyst's exercise of memory and desire:

If the psychoanalytic method is narrowly conceived of as consisting in the accumulation of knowledge (possessiveness), in harmony with the reality principle, and divorced from the processes of maturation and growth (either because growth is not recognised or because it is recognized but felt to be unattainable and beyond control of the individual), it becomes a potent stimulus for envy. (p. 48)

And finally that such reliance on memory and desire plays in with the patient's resistances:

> When the psychoanalyst anticipates some crisis, and especially if he has, or thinks he has, good grounds for anxiety, his tendency is to resort to memory and understanding to satisfy his desire for security ... This is understood by the psychotic patient, who does not resort to resistances but relies on being able to evoke the resistance-proliferating elements in his analyst; in other words, to stimulate the analyst's desires (notably for a successful outcome of the analysis), his memories and his understanding, thereby intending that his analyst's state of mind will not be open to the experience of which he might otherwise be a witness. (p. 51)

Before we leave this critique of Bion's views on the eschewing of memory and desire by the analyst, we must note the weaknesses in the foundations of the concept, for they will be dealt with to some extent later in the book. First of all, Bion has not yet distinguished between psychic reality and the unreal world of delusions and hallucinations. Second, he has only made a very weak attempt to explain why growth is so feared, which leaves one to assume that it is the possibility of regression and madness, not growth, which stirs the unbearable anxiety. His weak attempt is this: 'Of all the hateful possibilities, growth and maturation are feared and detested most frequently. This hostility to the process of maturation becomes most marked when maturation seems to involve the subordination of the pleasure principle ... the change from pleasure principle to reality principle does mean abandonment of control over the proportion of pain to pleasure' (p. 53). He will need to bring a more powerful concept to bear in order to harmonize the position of love for the truth as the driving force of development with this detestation of growth. But these weaknesses do not detract at this point from the overall harmony between this concept of the eschewing of memory and desire and Bion's model of the mind. The essential feature is his emphasis on the emotional experience and how the discovery of the truth about its nature is the food of the mind's growth. Everything that interferes with the rich 'perception' of the emotional experience weakens the capability of alpha-function to produce dream-thoughts suitable for thinking. Attention to, longing for, interest in, dwelling on, clinging to, ruminating over – all the many modes of preoccupation with past and future detract from the intensity of the experience of the moment and its perception. As this is the *sine qua non*, it is also the point at which resistance to change, in life and in analysis, directs its attack. Attention to the moment is requisite to its observation and for Bion the richness of thought is limited by the richness of observation. Hence his suspicion of number, so diametrically opposed to his valuing mathematical modes of thought.

CHAPTER THIRTEEN

The psychoanalytic couple and the group

The rounding out of Bion's views in *Attention and Interpretation* does not clearly declare itself until he begins to examine the relationship of the individual to the group. He means, in regard to the special problem of psychoanalysis, but perhaps to human relationships in general, the juxtaposition of the relations of individuals to one another as individuals to their involvements in group functions and mentality. The circling back to the work in *Experiences in Groups* shows again the internal integrity of Bion's life work and its progressive tightening and complexity, a fact which is superficially belied by the shifts in paraphernalia of exposition in the various major works. In the present book, where the language has shifted to the religious vocabulary, it is clear that the linguistic paraphernalia is the inevitable equipment of the religious vertex on the world. In *Elements* and *Transformations* Bion was inclined to hedge this with claims that the mathematical mode of expression was analogic rather than intrinsic. But in retrospect it is clear that he had a period of romance with a mathematical dream of a precise and quantifiable world of essential internal harmony threatened mainly by the failure of alpha-function, of containers to contain and of selected facts to be discovered to implement Ps↔D. It was not the case that he had abandoned the death instinct, the role of envy, innate destructiveness, etc. in his thought, but that the mathematical dream had no place in it for aught but confusion as the enemy of growth. In consequence the anti-growth elements in the mind could be relegated to a single 'use', column 2.

The failure of the mathematical vertex to contain the violence of emotionality of mental life and the impending explosion of that container of formulation when swollen with this fermenting stuff led to its abandonment in favour of the religious vertex. Thus the ultimate reality is no longer 'O' but 'God' and the striving to 'become O' is now the striving for direct contact with and fusion with God, while the person who claims to accomplish this is to be called the 'mystic'. The mutual need that exists between the mystic and the group that he belongs to, either in the constructive or destructive sense, is to be taken as the model for understanding the workings of psychoanalysis as a 'messianic idea', presumably one amongst many existing in the world but to be best investigated on the model of the most successful messianic idea of all time, the Christian one. While this seems to put psychoanalysis on a grand scale, and to place Bion in a self-aggrandizing position as the new Messiah, this would be a gross misunderstanding of his method of exposition. He is trying to investigate the workings of the psychoanalytical method using the tools he has devised, the Grid, container–contained, Ps–D and vertices. Words like 'messianic', 'god', 'establishment', 'explode', etc., carry what he would call the penumbra of bigness, importance. To understand him one must put this aside and think of little messiahs, little gods, little explosions as well. The question of size in cosmic terms is irrelevant. Quantity has really dropped away from his work. Everything is quality now, so it does not matter if it is psychoanalytical microbiology or psychoanalytical astronomy we think we are dealing with, the qualities are the same. It is the language of the religious vertex as a tool of investigation, a new model, not the trumpeting of the prophet. The problem in a sense is the same as used to be spoken of about aircraft and submarines, that they needed to be invented by geniuses so that they could be operated by idiots.

Taking the religious vertex Bion shows us a view of psychoanalysis that is of this sort, that great ideas exist in the world,
that they are discovered by thinkers and transmitted for use to
non-thinkers, for which purpose they must find a 'language',
not necessarily verbal, that can both contain the idea without
being exploded by its pressure of meaning nor be so rigid as to
compress the idea and thus reduce its meaningfulness. He wishes
to treat 'psycho-analysis' as a thing-in-itself which existed in the
world prior to its discovery by the mystic genius of Freud (big or
little does not matter) who gave it form in his writing and practice and teaching. From this arose, by virtue of this new thing
being uncontainable by the medical establishment, a new messianic establishment, eventually the International Psychoanalytic
Association, whose function was both evangelical and conserva-
tive. Upon this model of psychanalytical history the individual
practitioner becomes the idiot employing the equipment devised
by the genius, but must belong to an established society of
idiots who think they are geniuses because that society entitles
them to participate in the genius of a Freud, or Klein or Bion.
Without this form of participation they would not be able to
function in their consulting rooms to carry for their patients a
messianic genius significance which is essential to the work. Of
course this places them in danger of thinking themselves geniuses
or messiahs, but this is the industrial hazard of the job (talking
from the religious vertex, remember, for the sake of investigation and description). However, this establishment which confers
the sense of participation upon its members to enable them to
function with sincerity and conviction as psychoanalytical priests
administering the psychoanalytical sacraments (religious vertex,
not to be taken literally), also imposes upon them the conserva-
tism of the group, faithfulness to the old new-ideas and resistance
to new new-ideas, unless they can be proven to be implicit but
previously unnoticed in the gospels containing the old new-ideas.
These notions have their origin in Bion's earlier work on groups
in which there seemed implicit a tendency for the three basic
assumption groups to have a certain evolutionary sequence or
cycling to the effect: the pairing group eventually produces the
messianic leader and becomes the dependent group which
is embattled as the fight-flight group upon the leader's death

and must seek a new pair to gather its hope into. This then is the social-psychological setting of the practising psychoanalyst, viewed from the religious vertex, within which Bion wishes to investigate the operation of the individual, or rather the couple, analyst–analysand. His focus is on the requirements for making observations, for upon the accuracy and detail of this observation 'of the emotional experience' the richness of all subsequent mental processes and thus of growth depends. He has spent the first third of the book describing and limiting his dictum, which, voiced appropriately to the religious vertex, would read, 'Abandon your memory and your desire and your understanding and follow me' rather than 'Thou shalt not remember, thou shalt not desire, thou shalt not understand'. That is, New rather than Old Testament, exhortation rather than prohibition, as different from one another as 'Those who are not for me are against me' is from 'Those who are not against me are for me'. Bion quotes the latter. The inquisitor would have to quote the former. Bion presents himself as the mini-mystic of the psychanalytical group who claims that 'he comes not to destroy but to fulfil' the prior messianic messages of Freud and Melanie Klein. He is a new prophet of the 'mutative interpretation'. Taken in this way one can see that a 'process' view of psychoanalysis would serve as a comfort to the idiots that they need not really be geniuses in order to be sufficiently so apprehended by their patients that their interpretations, accurate or otherwise, precise or vague, may induce the 'catastrophic change' that is necessary for growth of the mind. From the religious vertex we practising idiots may reasonably be content to perform the rituals and sell our religious medals to induce in our patients the emergence of Faith that 'their redeemer liveth': that, in Melanie Klein's poetry, good internal objects exist – the acknowledgement of psychic reality.

But of course Bion is not himself content nor is he willing to encourage others to be content with being idiotic practitioners of psychoanalysis. He has discovered a way to creative work and is encouraging others to do the same, for them to practise what he thinks he has practised to achieve the 'beam of darkness' which can illuminate the non-sensuous world of psychic reality. He has found a formulation to express the tolerance of anxiety which is necessary to its accomplishment, found it in Keats's letter to his brothers in which he described the capacity to tolerate uncertainty, the 'negative capability' which he saw underlying the work of Shakespeare, whom he revered above all other writers.

But these exhortations to discipline do not really capture the essence of what Bion is describing, for he has already made it clear that to attain these ends it is necessary to withstand the 'frightful fiend' in oneself. This fiend he is able now to investigate in a richer way than beta-element or column 2 was able to suggest, than minus L or minus K could describe. He is now able to describe in full mystic richness the function of the liar in oneself. The glorious parable on page 100 captures the social context of political lying and makes the necessary rapprochement between his own theories, designated as row F, G or H, and those of Melanie Klein, designated as row C, myth or dream-thought.

> By contrast the feeble processes by which the scientists again and again attempted to support their hypotheses made it easy for the liars to show the hollowness of the pretensions of the upstarts and thus to delay, if not to prevent, the spread of doctrines whose effect could only have been to induce a sense of helplessness and unimportance in the liars and their beneficiaries. (p. 100)

This presentation of Melanie Klein's picture of the inner world makes it clear that the concreteness of psychic reality has the same texture as the concreteness of politics, that life and death of the mind are as much in the balance in the one as life and death of the culture 'and its beneficiaries' are in the other. Thus 'value' is at last brought into focus and prominence in Bion's work, but with the admission that 'If value is to be the criterion [for action based on decision] difficulty arises because there is no absolute value: the individual does not necessarily believe it is better to create than to destroy; a suicidal patient may seem to embrace the opposite view' (p. 101). One could add to that the pervert, the psychopath, the schizophrenic. They all behave as if they believed that it were better to destroy than create. This is the frightful fiend, the liar, the operator of H and minus K.

Still talking from the religious vertex and row C (Kleinian formulation) the struggle for development involves the taking of nourishing truth and avoiding poisonous lies; these nourishing truths are produced by good internal god-like objects while the poisonous lies are excreted by foul-fiendish devils in the self, or the two may become fused and con-fused to form the 'super'-ego. The decisions upon which the choice rests at any moment focuses on the choice between the risk of catastrophic change being induced by the messianic idea versus the preservation of a sense of power and importance by means of lies. This formulation will require, in terms of the grid format for the tabulation of thought processes, a negative grid, not merely column 2. Every category of the 'elements' of thought can be turned into a lie by the 'thinker'. Bion sees the manufacture of lies as an employment of positive ingenuity, while the achievement of truth is more passive, requiring submission to the operation of container and contained, the mechanism of Ps↔D under the vertex of L, K and, if possible F, where the value is placed on creating rather than destroying.

By thus distinguishing, from the religious vertex, between Paradise and Pandemonium (after Milton) Bion has finally made the necessary step of distinguishing between psychic reality and the world of lies, the delusional system. What has not yet been accomplished, but only hinted at or left unscathed by ineffectual sallies, is the source of the hatred of growth, other than the minus K of the 'frightful fiend', the minus L that is manifest in intolerance to pain and frustration. Bion has frequently hinted that this is related to what he calls 'catastrophic change' but is yet to illuminate. It is rather irritating to find that the only reference to it in the index says 'see Chapter 10' which does not in fact mention it. The brief mention of pre- and post-catastrophic states in *Transformations* was little help. The paper given to the British Psychoanalytic Society in 1966 and published in their bulletin is very little different from Chapter 12. Since it is central to the whole question of affects and mental pain, and thus is the mainspring of Bion's elaborated model of the mind, it will be used as the basis for summary in the final chapter. What remains to be discussed in this one is a question: did the introduction of the differentiation between parasitic, symbiotic and commensal modes of relationship between container and contained add to or at least enrich the model? And did the eventual formulation of 'patience' and 'security' as dimensions of the analyst's experience add anything to the investigation of the psycho-analytical method?

The attempt in Chapter 12 to transform the model of container–contained into one so flexible that it can serve to describe politics, the analytic situation and the structure of the personality hinges on the differentiation of thought and action in practice. Action can be the stable and customary actions which form the matrix of the container, say in the actions of the establishment in politics, of the habitual and stable actions of the patient or analyst in analysis. This container of actions must be flexible enough not to crush yet strong enough not to be destroyed by the new or messianic thought. The dogmatic must contain the messianic; the method must make thought possible in both analysand and analyst. But, he points out, the actions unavoidable even in communication always favour the preservation of the sense of power against the necessary experience of helplessness, negative capability. The uses of parasitic, symbiotic, commensal, do not appear, being based on biological models devoid of meaningfulness, to add to Bion's capacity to investigate the state of tension and conflict between the container and the messianic idea. He is driven back to Melanie Klein's descriptions of paranoid-schizoid and depressive positions, giving them a new operational slant under the designations 'patience' and 'security'. But he can go no further than Keats's negative criteria for 'patience' that it should be uncertainty 'without irritably reaching after fact and reason', while 'security' is the state enjoyed once the new pattern has 'evolved': 'I consider the experience of oscillation between "patience" and "security" to be an indication that valuable work is being achieved' (p. 124). The loaded words are 'valuable' in Ruskin's sense of 'life-giving' and 'achieved' in Keats's sense of 'man of achievement'. He finally falls back on the frightful fiend, envy: 'If the envy were to assume an aspect of whole object it could be seen as envy of the personality capable of maturation and of the object stimulating maturation' (p. 128). This is congruent with his view that attacks are essentially attacks on linking, a view in advance of Mrs Klein's formulation on envy. Envy, in Bion's view and in Bion's terms, would not be aroused either by container or contained but only by their successful (symbiotic) conjunction.

CHAPTER FOURTEEN

Review: catastrophic change and the mechanisms of defence

In order to bring to an end this study of the development of Bion's model of the mind, it is necessary to attempt to clarify the concept which is probably most central and least mentioned of all his ideas. Except for the paper titled 'Catastrophic change' which he read to the British Psychoanalytical Society in 1966, and which incidentally in its body never mentions the concept of the title, this phrase appears nowhere in the books. And yet all the books are about it, just as *Attention and Interpretation* is certainly about attention, although it is never mentioned in the text. The paper 'Catastrophic change' was a prelude to *Attention* and is virtually identical to Chapter 12. In so far as its focus is upon the relationship of container and contained, in the individual and in his relationship to the group, the dread of change and the tendency for change to manifest itself as catastrophe is brought out more clearly than in the later book chapter entitled 'Container and contained transformed'. Bion's model of container and contained must be juxtaposed to his idea that the truth does not require a thinker to exist, but rather that the thinker needs to find the truth as an idea which he can make

grow in his mind. Among the ideas which exist in the world
awaiting thinkers are certain ones which, from the religious-
historical vertex, he chooses to call 'messianic' ideas. The relationship of container to contained in the individual, in so far
as ideas institute a conflict between thought and the impulse
to action, is not so observable in the ordinary course of events,
but becomes dramatically manifest when an idea of messianic significance enters. In order to describe these processes
of catastrophic change induced by the messianic idea Bion
employs the congruent relationship of the individual mystic
to his group. The group, as container, must find some means
of expanding to hold this new phenomenon in order, on the
one hand, not to crush or squeeze or denude the messianic
idea, or similarly to destroy the mystic or 'sink him without
a trace, loaded with honours'. But it also must avoid being
fragmented or exploded by the mystic or the messianic idea.
These relations of container to contained, whether of experiences in the individual, the individual in a group, the meaning in a word, the significance in a symbol, or the passion
in a relationship – in whatever dimension of container and
contained, the relationship can be categorized as parasitic,
symbiotic or commensal. His application of these biological
ideas to the realm of the mind is this:

> *Commensal* – the thought O and the thinker exist quite
> independently of each other. There is no reaction, or, as we
> should ordinarily say identifying ourselves with the thinker,
> the truth has not been discovered even though it 'exists'.
>
> *Symbiotic* – the thought and the thinker correspond and
> modify each other through the correspondence. The thought
> proliferates and the thinker develops.
>
> *Parasitic* – Thought and thinker correspond but the cor-
> respondence is category [i.e. column] 2, meaning that the
> formulation is known to be false but is retained as a barrier
> against a truth which is feared as annihilating to the con-
> tainer or vice versa.

> (*Scientific Bulletin* of the British Psychoanalytical Society
> no. 5, 1966, p. 21)

A 'critical situation' is said to develop when the commensal approaches the symbiotic, as a 'discovery' threatens. The 'critical situation' calls up the image of atomic reactors.

This then is the prototype of anxiety in the Bionic model of the mind, and it can be seen that this catastrophic anxiety lurks behind all lesser anxieties. It is what would be 'signalled' by Freud's final conceptualization, 'signal anxiety'. It would underlie the mental pains of the paranoid-schizoid and depressive positions of Mrs Klein's model; it would correspond to Mrs Bick's 'dead end' and 'endless falling' and 'liquefaction'; to Bion's own formulation in *Learning* of 'nameless dread'; or my own delineation of 'terror' of dead objects. It is perhaps the 'moment of truth' of the bullfight with its many levels of symbolic reference, good and evil, male and female, life and death, Christian and Pagan, human and animal. It is clear that Bion sees the 'absolute truth, O' as not containable, requiring some degree of falsification to be held within the individual mind. Only the mystic claims to hold or behold it, but even he cannot communicate (publish) it without some degree of falsification. It is the degree and the motive for falsification that makes the difference between the truth that can be contained and allowed to grow in the mind and the lie which destroys the truth and replaces it with 'morality'.

Having now described the crucial aspect of Bion's ideas as they lend themselves to employment in the psychoanalytical consulting room, it should be possible to review the history of the evolution of the model of the mind which underlies our practice, as it has progressed in the line of the 'Kleinian Development' from Freud through Klein to Bion. It is of course too big a task for this context but the method of approach and an outline of the general scheme should be possible. It is proposed, therefore, to review the salient features of the model of the mind implicit or explicit in the writings, particularly the clinical ones, of all three and to see what these different models imply with respect to the concept 'mechanisms of defence' – assuming that all the areas of psychopathology which reveal themselves through the transference in analysis are based upon defence against anxiety. It may not be true, and perhaps one of the advances implicit in Bion's work is an approach to other areas of pathology, but it can be said with certainty that psychoanalysts unanimously assume that they are studying 'defence neuro-psychoses', to use Freud's earliest term.

Freud's eventual model of the mind, as defined in papers such as 'The ego and the id', 'Beyond the pleasure principle', 'The problem of anxiety', and 'Splitting of the ego in the service of defence' probably goes something like this: an undifferentiated mass of psychic energy, both creative and destructive, finds its manifestation in the mental representations of the id, which the ego, having evolved from the id and having developed a capacity, consciousness, for the perception of psychic qualities, seeks to put into action in the world in order to reduce tension to a minimum. But to the complexities inherent in the conflict of life and death instincts there is added the task of serving or evading the demands of the real world and of an internal institution, the super-ego derived from childhood relation to parents and variously modified by later experiences with figures of dependence, authority and admiration. In this plight, 'serving three masters', the ego resorts to various devices: interposing thought between impulse and action; actions to modify external reality; hallucinatory wish fulfilment and the mechanisms of defence. These latter serve to modify the signal anxiety engendered by conflict in the ego aroused by the incompatible demands of its various 'masters'. The development of the ego, its psycho-sexual development, consists of a series of stages, partly determined by the maturation of the physical organism and partly by increasing and varied demands of the environment, whereby the leading erogenous zone of contact, the nature of the object and the aim of relationship progress from primary narcissism to genitality.

Under this model psychoanalytic practice tends to confine itself to areas of disturbance beyond the narcissistic stages, where ambivalence to part- and whole-objects in the outside world are aggravated by harshness of the demands and threats emanating from the super-ego. Its method is to study the free associations, to relieve resistances by investigation of the transference, and to interpret dreams in order that a reconstruction of the development of the disturbance may be achieved and worked through with the patient, thus relieving the repressions, abating the perversions and enabling psychosexual development to proceed. Mechanisms of defence, which correspond in many ways to the 'dream work' that transforms the unacceptable latent content into a manifest content acceptable to the dream censor (?super-ego) are relinquished by the patient once they are made conscious, if by so doing the economic interplay of pleasure and reality principles is facilitated rather than aggravated. The list of mechanisms of defence, headed by repression, projection, introjection, denial, negation, isolation of affects and splitting of the ego, is open to new members as they are described. But mechanisms are named for their manifestations; the actual mechanism, probably at base chemical or neurophysiological, is not observable but can only be construed with uncertainty.

Freud's model of the mind is an explanatory model of a mechanical causal system aimed at explaining deviations in normal development and functioning as a basis for therapy. It is not a system of psychology for describing the life of the mind, although it rests upon observations of phenomena and not in any way upon neurophysiological or neuroanatomical facts. Melanie Klein's explicit model of the mind is completely Freudian, but the model implicit in her clinical descriptions is quite different. It is not an explanatory model of a causal system but a description of the geography of phantasy life in which a theatre for the generating of meaning is found to exist 'inside' the mind whereby the forms of the external world can be imbued with meaning and emotional significance. It is a model that emphasizes development which is seen to commence shortly after birth through the baby's experiences with the mother, or first with her breast. By means of splitting the self and object into good and bad, and by phantasies of introjection and projective identification, implemented by a sense of omnipotence, the baby constructs from its gratifying and frustrating experiences an internal world of objects and parts of the self in which its unconscious phantasies and dreams manipulate the meaning and emotional significance of its experiences. These then serve as its model for construing its experiences, and consequently regulating its behaviour, with objects in the outside world. Since it assumes that external objects also have an internal world as concrete as its experience of its own, its 'world', which at first is the body of its mother, is the object of its epistemophilic instinct in respect of both its exterior and interior qualities. The life and death instincts of the id manifest themselves in the emotional impulses which arise from gratifying and frustrating events, namely love and hate, much complicated by envy in the two-body relation, later augmented by jealousy in the three-body or Oedipal situations. Bad objects, bad parts of the self and objects damaged by its omnipotent attacks in the internal and external world engender persecutory anxieties which it variously defends against by splitting processes, projective identification, denial of psychic reality and dependence upon good or idealized objects, all implemented in unconscious phantasy and action with varying degrees of omnipotence. When love and dependence upon good objects grows to a certain point, solicitude for its own safety and comfort tends to give way to concern for the welfare of its loved objects and a new system of values or economic principle: the depressive position, is ushered in. In so far as it can maintain a depressive orientation, development through the reintegration of splitting of self and objects takes place, omnipotence is gradually relinquished and schizoid mechanisms are abandoned in favour of trust and dependence upon internal objects and those figures in the outside world who carry the transference from these internal ones. Progress from part-object to whole-object relationships strengthens the internal situation and identification with internal objects enables the ego to grow in strength, while reintegration of its splitting amplifies the complexity of the mental functions it can manage. An adult part of the personality, developed through its introjective identifications, assumes more control of its relations to the outside world while its infantile relationships are more and more confined to internal objects, thus lessening the tendency to transference.

Under this model psychoanalytical therapy is mainly aimed at making possible a re-experiencing of the essence of the developmental process through the transference, its evolution being facilitated by interpretation. It is essentially a corrective developmental experience in which reintegration of split-off parts of self and objects is facilitated by achievement of the depressive position. But the goodness of this experience may even modify the virulence of the death instinct as it is represented in attitudes of envy and their interference with the development of gratitude and thus of love. As a model for use in scientific investigation it is quite powerful in the investigation of object relations and narcissistic organizations. The mechanisms of defence completely lose their mechanistic quality and neurophysiological foundation, become infinite in variety since they are unconscious phantasies implemented with omnipotence. For the sake of description they are gathered under the headings of schizoid mechanisms (splitting and projective identification), manic mechanisms (denial of psychic reality) and obsessional mechanisms (omnipotent control and separation of objects).

The world described by Melanie Klein's model of the mind is a world of emotional relationships, full of meaning, value and significance as categories of experience but has no direct means of describing man as a thinking creature in a world of other individual thinking creatures. It can describe intimate relationships but not the world of casual and contractual ones.

If Freud's world is one of creatures seeking surcease from the constant bombardment of stimuli from inside and out, a world of higher animals; and Melanie Klein's world in one of holy babes in holy families plagued by the devils of split-off death instinct; Bion's world is one of the questing mind seeking the absolute truth with inadequate equipment. Like Freud he sees the mind in isolation, but struggling to free itself from the protomental level of basic assumption group-life, and yet needing the group for survival and perpetuation of its discoveries of the truth. Like Melanie Klein he sees the mind as developing in the context of the infant–mother relationship but for him it is a relationship whose essence is understanding rather than gratification, failure of such understanding rather than frustration. The growth of the mind is not, as in Freud, the natural realization of innate processes, all going well; nor, like Melanie Klein's is it a process of complicated unfolding given sufficient nurturing and protection; it is rather seen by Bion as the growth of the capacity for thinking about emotional experiences which enable the individual to learn by becoming a different person with different capabilities from the person of the past. The life of the individual is in the moment of his being himself having experiences and thinking about them, the past and the future being hindrances in so far as he is living in them rather than in the present. Nothing described by Freud or Melanie Klein is thus replaced by Bion's model, but would be relegated to row F (scientific deductive system about man as intelligent animal) and row C (the mind's mythology about itself and its origins) respectively. Neither would be seen as incorrect or irrelevant, but variously incomplete and inadequate for certain clinical (and philosophical) tasks.

Bion's model of the mind as a thinking and learning apparatus is concerned with understanding the emotional experiences that impinge upon it as it watches them in its head with its capacity for selective attention through its organ of consciousness for the perception of psychic qualities, like Plato's cave-dwellers. It has an apparatus for converting these emotional experiences into thoughts that can be used for thinking, that is for manipulation with a view to increasing their level of abstraction and sophistication. This apparatus (alpha-function) it had introjected as a breast during infancy; a breast that was able to receive the baby's projective identifications of parts of itself in chaotic distress of bombardment by emotional experiences, accompanied by the fear that it was dying; and could furthermore divest these parts of their distress, order their chaos and return them to the baby in a state equivalent to having phantasies or dreams. This form of communication by projective identification continues to be available in later relationships but, in order to communicate anything other than a state of mind, more abstract means, employing signs and symbols are required, and in order to form them from the row C elements (unconscious phantasy) a similar system of containment and interaction of the container with its contents of thoughts is evolved through identification with this introjected breast. If this containment is possible: that is, if the mind can hold a new idea without compressing its meaning and without being disrupted by it; if it can bear the stirrings of catastrophic anxiety engendered, it can bring to bear a movement from a paranoid-schizoid value set to a depressive orientation to the new idea which, with the help of a selected fact to organize the new with older ideas, enables growth of the idea to take place. By this means, if truth is loved, it can grow and be digested and nourish the mind by learning from experience. But if the truth is hated or if the anxiety is evaded or if the apparatus is defective, lies, the poison of the mind, may eventuate instead. These lies are probably of three sorts: emotional experiences not changed into thoughts (beta-elements), thoughts degraded by the apparatus for growth of thought (alpha-function) working in reverse, or possibly by an identical negative apparatus operated by a 'frightful fiend' part of the personality. By this last means experiences may be turned into lies that can be used for constructing a world of unreality, the delusional system and hallucinosis.

Operating with this model of the mind, the psychoanalyst would conceive of his task as one dedicated to sharing with the patient the emotional experience of the moment, seeking, as the mother with the baby, to receive in reverie the projective identifications, etc. But he would also aim to facilitate the growth of new ideas by offering his opinion at levels of abstraction and sophistication above the level of myth or dream thought. His capacity to function in this way would be limited by his ability to free himself from concern with the past and future of the relationship and his tolerance of the catastrophic anxiety he would need to share with the patient.

In the Bionic model mechanisms of defence are various forms of lies, embracing those described by Melanie Klein but also lies at a more sophisticated and abstract level. In addition various forms of failure of the apparatus could be studied which are not merely mechanisms of defence against anxiety but disorders of the capacity to think, of attacks upon the capacity for thought, and of attempts to live in a world of anti-thought. In so far as group life, with its roots in protomental phenomena at a level in which emotion and bodily experiences and events are indistinguishable, stands in conflict with the individual's capacity to learn from experience, Bion's model of the mind opens up to observation and study an area of conflict previously not noted or attended to but relegated to the category of acting out. Seen as a model superimposed upon those of Freud and Melanie Klein, Bion's model would seem to open a vast area of phenomena to the psychoanalyst which he has not previously had the conceptual tools to observe and consider. This vast area could reasonably be called the area of mindlessness in mental life, one of which, autism, my colleagues and I have begun to explore. Bion's concepts proved useful for deepening understanding of the element of mindlessness in obsessional phenomena, in fetishism and in two-dimensional areas of object relations. Mrs Bick, in parallel with Bion, can be seen to have been studying phenomena of failure of primary containment and its effects upon the personality when 'second skin' manoeuvres are employed to augment the defective containment. Perhaps it would not be too optimistic to say that Bion's work has broadened the scope of psychoanalysis in the same exponential proportions that Mrs Klein's work can be seen in retrospect to have done. These elevations of Freud's work to the third power, so to speak, have enabled psychoanalysis to grow from a narrow therapy of the neuroses and perversions, marred by overweening ambitions to explain everything, to a scientific method which may prove to be adequate to investigate and describe everything and explain nothing.

A note on Bion's concept 'reversal of alpha-function'[1]

When a new theory is proposed in psychoanalysis it can be said to undertake two functions: one is to organize the clinical phenomena that have already been observed in a more aesthetic (beautiful?) way; the other is to provide a tool of observation that will open to view previously invisible phenomena of the consulting room. Wilfred Bion, beginning with his papers on schizophrenia, sought to amplify the model of the mind which we employ in psychoanalysis so that processes of thinking and disturbances in this capacity could be investigated. The first systematic presentation of this effort, *Learning from Experience* (1962) formulated an 'empty' concept of alpha-function by means of which the 'sense impressions of emotional experiences' were converted into elements to be used in various ways: as building-blocks for dream thoughts which could in turn be used for thinking; to be available for storage as memory; and by their continuity, to form a 'contact barrier' that might separate conscious from unconscious mental processes.

---

1   First published in *Festschrift for W. R. Bion*, ed. J. Grotstein. New York: Aronson, 1978.

The 'emptiness' of this model was stressed over and over by Bion, along with the caution against over-hasty attempts to fill it with clinical meaning. He himself has been almost single-handedly exploring its possible meaning in the series of books which followed, namely *Elements of Psychoanalysis, Transformations*, and *Attention and Interpretation*. It is with a certain trepidation that this paper is offered as a tentative exploration of his fascinating idea that alpha-function can perhaps operate in reverse, cannibalizing the already formed alpha-elements to produce either the beta-screen or perhaps bizarre objects. It is probably best to quote rather than to paraphrase. He writes, in evaluating the analyst's and patient's separate contributions to the situation in which the beta-screen is being formed: 'The analysand contributes changes which are associated with the replacement of alpha-function by what may be described as a reversal of direction of the function'. (*Learning from Experience*, p. 25). And here he adds a note:

> The reversal of direction is compatible with the treatment of thoughts by evacuation; that is to say, that if the personality lacks the apparatus that would enable it to "think" thoughts but is capable of attempting to rid the psyche of thoughts in much the same way as it rids itself of accretions of stimuli, then reversal of alpha-function may be the method employed.

He continues:

> Instead of sense impressions being changed into alpha elements for use in dream thoughts and unconscious waking thinking, the development of the contact-barrier is replaced by its destruction. This is effected by the reversal of alpha-function so that the contact barrier and the dream thoughts and unconscious waking thinking, which are the texture of the contact-barrier, are turned into alpha-elements, divested of all characteristics that separate them from beta-elements and are then projected, thus forming the beta-screen.

Further, 'Reversal of alpha-function means the dispersal of the contact-barrier and is quite compatible with the establishment of objects with the characteristics I once ascribed to bizarre objects.'

He further points out that there is an important difference in his conception of the beta-element and the bizarre object: the latter is 'beta-element plus ego and superego traces'.

Before we can embark upon the clinical material through which meaning may be poured into the 'empty' vessel of thought, it is necessary to remind the reader of an historical item. Bion has amplified Melanie Klein's concept of sadistic and omnipotent attacks upon internal objects and the structure of the self to include also attacks on individual functions of the ego and upon 'linking' in general as the basic operation in thought, its prototype being the link between infant and breast. To test the usefulness of Bion's formulations it is necessary to demonstrate that they make possible an integration of observations not possible by previous formulations. The particular question that will arise in connection with the material to follow is this: does the formulation of alpha-function and its possible reversal extend the range of psychoanalytic observation and thought beyond that made possible by Mrs Klein's formulations regarding sadistic attacks, splitting processes and projective identification with internal objects?

Clinical material – a 35-year-old man

The session begins perhaps two minutes late: no comment. He has had a horrible dream, which it takes him some considerable time to tell against strong resistance, in the form of a 'what's the use' attitude. The background of the dream collects before the dream is actually presented, including some material of previous sessions which had dealt with his feelings of ingratitude to his mother's friends whom the two of them had visited in Germany in the summer. He had never sent a thank-you note but yesterday had received an invitation for Christmas. He hates ingratitude in himself or others and yesterday' s material had centred on a fellow of the college (his initials D.M.) whose furniture the patient had helped to move; D.M. has never thanked the patient nor invited him to dinner. Today's material then veers off into a description of his sensitivity to his surroundings and how he will lose his room in college next year and have to find one in another which he hates. It is connected with the institute in the U.S.A. where he spent two miserable years and he also feels at loggerheads with X who tried to bully him into accepting the 'great honour' of being a fellow at his college.

In the dream there is a huge L-shaped room like one at the American institute hut also, by virtue of the grey lino, like his present room, as it was before he had bullied and cajoled the authorities into carpeting and decorating. He had also exchanged all the horrible furniture for a rather nice settee and chairs. Yes, he realizes that this excessive dependence on external comfort implies a defect in his internal sense of security. In the dream *someone was talking about an old woman who had been dreadfully deformed by an accident. Then she seemed to be there on the floor, alive but so deformed she was hardly recognitable as a human. One extraordinary and somehow particularly horrible feature was that originally she had had extremely long fingernails, extending not only outward but also up her fingers, and under the skin of the arm. These seemed to have been struck and driven up her arm so that their ends stuck out near her elbows. The point seemed to be that she was suing for compensation but this was refused on the ground that she was so completely deformed that one could get no idea at all of what had been her original state. This applied particularly to the fingernails, for, although they did not protrude from her fingers but only from her elbows, the intervening nails did not show through the skin. The impression of horror did not seem to be accompanied by any emotion other than aversion.* I suggest to him that the background of the dream indicates that the problem is one of guilt and reparation, neither of which can be set in motion unless the mutilated object can be recognized and connected with its former undamaged and perhaps young and beautiful state, i.e. his mother as a young woman in his childhood as compared with the old woman, equated with her friends in Germany, who kept being generous to him despite his ingratitude, thus becoming old and empty. In order to get rid of this tormenting sense of guilt it is necessary to so attack the old mother that her disfigurement defies connection with the original object, thus becoming 'some old woman' rather than 'mummy'. But is there not a mathematical technique that he mentioned yesterday, called 'transpositional equations', connected with analytical geometry, whereby, if the distortion of the grid of reference can be demonstrated, two objects which seem grossly different can be shown to be basically identical but projected on to different grid systems like distortions in a picture on a piece of rubber? He agrees; his work deals with the mathematics which makes such crude analogies unnecessary. (I am thinking of the pictures of fish and skulls in D'Arcy Thompson's *Growth of Form* and he confirms this reference.) The long fingernails therefore represent the lines of the grid and if they can be made visible and the grid rectified to its basic axes, the image of the beautiful young mother can be rediscovered in the dehumanized old woman. The motto of the defence would be, 'If you damage mummy and the sight of it causes you guilt and remorse, smash her beyond all recognition until you feel only horror and revulsion'.

Discussion

We were approaching the first holiday break of this man's analysis, which had been arranged at an interview just prior to the previous summer holiday when he was expecting his mother to come all the way from Australia to visit him and take him to see some aristocratic friends of hers in Germany. The patient had not seen his mother for some years and was disturbed, not only at finding her looking much older than his image of her, but also at finding his prior devotion much cooled. He is the eldest of her children and the only 'successful' one, having been rather arrogantly independent since early childhood.

From the Kleinian point of view it is a rather ordinary dream that illustrates the thesis that retreat from depressive anxiety referrable to damaged internal objects follows a route whereby the depressive pain is felt as persecutory depression and opens the way to further attacks on the damaged object as a persecutor. The parallel material of his associations suggests that the room in college which he had made cosy by 'bullying and cajoling' the authorities to carpet, hiding the old lino which reminded him of the 'two miserable years' in the United States, was to be taken away: that is, that the analysis was threatening to return him to a state of misery (the analyst being from the U.S.) as revenge for his not feeling 'honoured' at being accepted for analysis (as with X's invitation). The analyst, like the fellow with the same initials (D.M.), is to contain the split-off attribute of ingratitude.

But what could a Kleinian formulation make of these finger-nails which, instead of growing out, had been driven in the reverse direction until they stuck out at the old woman's elbow? What could it make of the refusal of compensation on the grounds that the old woman was so horribly deformed that no idea could be established of her previous state? Perhaps we can assume that the imponderable nature of the deformed old woman is exactly the quality that makes her a bizarre object in Bion's sense rather than a mutilated object in Mrs Klein's. In the courtroom of the dream no one seemed to doubt that she had been a human, that there had been an accident, that her fingernails had been driven up her arm. But somehow the frame of reference of thought had been destroyed, a frame having a particular connection with the patient's overriding professional preoccupations. One might say that his work has to do with getting to the truth about problems of analytical geometry through formulae which would be far more precise than the 'crude analogies, of grid-distortion.

Not only could Kleinian formulations before Bion have made no headway with such a problem; they would not have been able even to state the problem itself: namely the attack on thinking. They could approach only the attack on feeling, where, of course, they go quite some distance. In contrast a Freudian formulation would probably focus attention on the castration anxiety, which is most certainly an element in the dream (are the woman's nipples the remnants of her penis, smashed up and driven inward and upward until they stick out of the breasts?).

Bionic recapitulation

The patient is facing the first holiday break of his analysis and feels that his jealousy of the other analytical children is going to drive him to attack his internal analytical mother with a view to lessening the devotion and its consequent separation pain. But the return to analysis would hold him to a state of mind of misery about these attacks, hating himself for ingratitude, perhaps even reducing him to having to beg, rather than bully, the daddy-authorities to redecorate the mummy and make her cosy once more. That would be unbearably humiliating to such an inde-pendent baby. Although he has spent years developing a mode of thought for seeing the truth with precision in such situations, he is prepared to destroy that mental capacity (alpha-function of a particular sort) by making it run in reverse (instead of growing outward to form the lines of a grid of reference, the fingernails are driven backwards to disappear under the skin, appearing only at the elbows). The consequence is a beta-element 'plus ego and superego traces' (the distorted old woman, having only traces of the mother and of his discarded ego-capacity for thinking with transpositional equations). She is now a bizarre object, uncontainable in thought, suitable only for evacuation.

Implications

Let us take the 'crude analogy' of a geometric grid on a piece of rubber as a model of a piece of mental equipment, a particular bit of alpha-function apparatus. Place on it a picture of an old woman and pull the rubber in various ways until the picture of a beautiful young woman appears. Take this as a model of alpha-function operating on 'the sense impressions of an emotional experience'. Such a bit of apparatus may be essential for the creation of an image that makes it possible to connect the old woman who visits the patient from Australia with the young beautiful mother who insisted on having other children against his sage advice.

Postscript

The analysis progressed very well through the next term bringing forward memory after memory of the catastrophic reactions to the births of his next siblings, reactions which progressively relegated his father to a position of negligible importance in his life and consolidated his status as mother's little husband and advisor. As the second holiday break approached he became rather restive, left early to go to Australia to visit his family on the grounds that his next sibling (who had the same Christian name as the analyst) needed his help and advice. While there he did a group-therapy 'experience' during which he developed a manic state, thought he was the Messiah, and returned late to break off the analysis, full of 'gratitude' that the analysis had laid the background for his total cure in the group. He was, however, willing to see the analyst once a week to help him, that is, the analyst, understand how this transformation had come about. Over the next two months he gradually slipped into a state of depression after breaking off completely in a rage at the analyst's 'stupidity'. He finally returned to analysis in time to make a more satisfactory preparation for the long summer break. It was of interest that he could not bring himself to pay his fees until the last day, by which time the four months of work came to almost the precise amount he had paid for the five-day group 'therapy'.

Dr Bion wrote me a kind and interesting note when I sent him the paper:

> 'aesthetic (beautiful) way' – Now I would use as a model: the diamond cutter's method of cutting a stone so that a ray of light entering the stone is reflected back by the same path in such a way that the light is augmented – the same 'free association' is reflected back by the same path, but with augmented 'brilliance'. So the patient is able to see his 'reflection', only more clearly than he can see his personality as expressed by himself alone [i.e. without an analyst].

INDEX

Abraham, K. 31, 71
acting/acting out 10, 93, 125
aesthetic experience 79, 80, 81,
    83, 92, 98, 103, 127, 134
  not in Grid 72
affects, theory of 42, 67, 114
alpha-function 23, 34, 37ff, 56,
    76, 91, 124
  and beta-elements 44–45, 87
  and conscious/unconscious
    40, 51, 82, 84
  and container–contained 47,
    61, 103
  digestive analogy 52, 56
  elements 69
  'empty' concept 38, 39, 40
  failure of 110
  and LHK 47, 52, 68
  operates on perception 40, 41
  and projective identification
    48
  vs. 'super'-ego

reverse of 53, 127ff
  transformations in 78, 97
  and truth 50
    see also symbol formation
anxiety 13, 20, 67, 68, 107, 112,
    119, 125, 131
  castration 132
  and catastrophic change 119,
    124
  dying, fear of 34, 52, 53,
  nameless dread 53, 98, 119
  optimal level 87
  persecutory 32
  signal theory (Freud) 68
  in structural model 102
    see also mental pain
attention 59, 60, 99, 108
  free-floating 81, 104, 105
  selective 124
autism 66, 71, 89, 125
basic assumption groups 7–8, 13,
    91, 123

dependent 7
evolutionary sequence of 111
flight-flight 14, 111
messianic leader 111
pairing 9
vs. work group 9, 14
beta-elements 40, 44–45, 63, 113, 124
  beta-screen 95, 128
  and non-existence 87
  pathological 50, 53, 68
  plus ego and superego traces 128, 133
Bick, E. 71, 119, 125
binocular vision 3, 4, 5, 8, 13, 15, 47, 51
  and reality testing 81, 82, 84, 85, 88, 92
Bion, W. R., writings
  'Attacks on linking' 30,
  Attention and Interpretation 51, 91, 93, 97, 99, 100, 109, 117, 128
  'Catastrophic change' 63, 117, 118
  'Development of schizophrenic thought' 19ff
  'Differentiation of the psychotic from the non-psychotic personalities' 35
  Elements of Psychoanalysis 48, 55ff, 65, 70, 73, 76, 81, 83, 85, 88, 91, 104, 109
  Experiences in Groups 1ff, 11, 109
  'Group dynamics: a review' 11ff
  'The imaginary twin' 16–18
  Learning from Experience 17, 29, 34, 37, 38, 47, 127, 128
  A Memoir of the Future 102

'Notes on the theory of schizophrenia' 19ff
'On arrogance' 30, 31
'On hallucination' 26, 27, 34
Second Thoughts 10
'A theory of thinking' 30, 34
Transformations 54, 75ff, 83, 91, 92, 97, 100, 104, 109, 114, 128
bizarre objects 24, 27, 33, 34, 43, 45, 50, 68, 79, 98, 128
  vs. non-existent 86
  vs. no-things 88
breast, as object 31, 32, 34, 124
  absent/no-breast 52, 84, 88
  baby's preconception of 52
  and container-contained 47, 54, 61, 63
  and dependent group 14
  envy of 53
  first link 32, 33, 38
  and nipple 16
  no-breast 52
  see also container–contained; object
catastrophic anxiety 105, 119
catastrophic change 93, 96, 112, 117ff
  and messianic idea 114
  as transformation in O 93
common sense 17, 50, 58, 82
communication
  external/internal 78
  intra-disciplinary 48
  mother-child 33
  non-verbal 70
  projective identification as 52, 68, 124
  psychoanalytical 20, 55, 81, 84, 91, 100, 115
  'publication' 85
consciousness, role of 8, 23, 33,

38, 87, 102
as organ of perception 34, 40,
    120, 124
contact barrier (conscious/uncon-
    scious) 40, 42, 47, 50, 82, 84,
    127, 128
container–contained 47ff
    commensal/parasitic/symbi-
        otic modes 118
    and K 53–54
    and new idea 54, 111, 124
    and Ps↔D 56
    skin as (Bick) 71
countertransference 12, 23, 30,
    77, 96, 98, 102
    see also transference
curiosity 32, 84, 105
    see also knowledge
death instinct 32, 33, 39, 110,
    120, 121, 122, 123
defence mechanisms 14, 27, 50,
    101, 119–121, 123, 125,
    131
delusional system 27, 86, 88, 92,
    105, 107, 125
    and anti-grid 92
    and lies 98, 114
    recovery phase 22
    Schreber case 22, 38
depressive position 21, 32, 35, 66,
    106, 122
    and paranoid-schizoid oscilla-
        tion Ps↔D 56, 61, 65, 71
dream(s), in analysis 10, 17, 31,
    66, 78, 85, 120
    vs. hallucination 27, 102
    meaning of 42
    -myth 67–68, 125
    -thoughts 39, 40, 42, 52, 59,
        69, 78, 103, 113, 128
elements of psychoanalysis 34, 39,
    55ff, 66, 70, 72, 83, 127
    see also beta-elements

emotion(s)
    conflict (LHK) 47, 49, 58,
        66, 72, 78
    hatred of 33, 38, 53
    mythical apparatus for 39
    processing of 39–40, 43–44,
        52, 67, 82, 124, 127
    representation of 50, 56, 68,
        93, 121
    and mental life/pain 41, 49,
        54, 68, 101, 110, 124
    observable facts 83
    and things-in-themselves 63
    see also passion
envy 52, 53, 106, 122
    as 'fiend' 115
epistemophilic instinct see knowl-
    edge, thirst for
'fiend' part of personality 104,
    105, 106, 113, 114, 115,
    125
Freud, A. 20
Freud, S. passim
    consciousness as organ 34
    ego and id 41, 52, 62, 120
    group psychology 8, 14
    jigsaw method 42
    and models of the mind 22,
        27, 43, 53, 71, 102, 120
    primary and secondary pro
        cess 42, 44, 50
    Schreber case 22, 37, 86
    two principles of mental func
        tioning 23
Glover, E. 25
Grid 56–61, 66, 83–88, 92
    absence of 'aesthetic' 72, 80
    and anti-/negative grid 92,
        114
    and growth of thoughts
        65–68, 70–71
Grinberg, L. 12

groups 1ff,
    conflict in 9
    and individual 13, 109, 117,
        118
    and messianic idea 114
    and mystic 93, 110, 112
    primitive mentality in 8, 14,
        91
    re-viewed 11
        see also basic assumption
            groups; work group
growth, mental 50, 53, 54, 61,
        78–80, 94, 98, 112
    in analyst 104
    anti- 110, 114
    Bion's view *vs.* Freud, Klein
        103, 123
    fear of 107
    of meaning/thoughts (Grid)
        65–67, 83, 88
    with selected fact 3, 61, 63,
        65, 72, 110, 124
hallucinosis 92–93, 101, 105, 125
hate (H) *see* emotions, conflict
Heimann, Paula 12
hypothesis, definatory 59, 81
identification processes 6, 7
    with group 8
    introjective 122
    projective *see* projective iden-
        tification
        see also introjection
inner/internal world 22, 42, 51,
        86, 98, 113, 121
    and external 43
    vs. delusional 92
    as mental spaces 42, 64, 88
    source of meaning 43, 81, 86
        see also reality, psychic
integration
    depressive orientation 33,
        103, 122

and disintegration 61, 62, 63,
        72, 79, 94
interpretation, role of 20, 56, 80,
        94, 96, 103, 112, 122
    mutative 15, 112
    as psychoanalytical object 66,
        69, 78
introjection 24, 33, 43, 52, 103,
        121, 124
Isaacs, Susan 42
Kant, Immanuel 60, 93
Keats, John 82, 104, 112, 115
Klein, M.
    on early transference 77
    model of mind 80, 104, 123
    the positions 21, 61–62, 65,
        71, 80, 85, 88, 115, 119
    on projective identification
        22, 33, 39, 129
    on unconscious phantasy 26,
        31, 42, 68
    'Notes on some schizoid
        mechanisms' 12, 19, 39
knowledge, search for 21, 34, 43,
    and hubris 32, 38
    K link (truth) 49, 84, 92, 94
    minus K 49, 53, 62, 84, 87,
        92, 93, 94, 95, 113
    and new idea/thought 98,
        111, 114
    self- 2
    tree of 66
    unknowing, cloud of 63
        see also emotions, conflict;
        O; truth
language
    Bion's use of 2, 3, 11, 15, 16,
        28, 70, 94, 109
    for new idea 111
    as notational system 85
    philosophy of 21, 96, 100
learning from experience 1, 9, 35,

42, 49, 124
vs. learning about 54, 93
vs. parasitism 77, 118
see also knowledge
lies/liar 52, 92, 98, 113, 114, 124,
    125
links
    attacks on 27, 30, 72, 82,
        115
    emotional (LHK) 47, 49, 58,
        66, 72, 78
    see also vertices
madness, fear of 95, 106, 107
maternal reverie 52, 98, 125
meaning
    and aesthetic experience 81
    breast, as container 84
    and empty concepts 48, 53,
        46, 66, 71, 128
    and new idea 111, 118, 124
    and geography of phantasy
        (Klein) 103, 121
    infinite possibilities 89, 98
    vs. signs 62
    and thinking 68, 69, 83, 87,
        88
    premature attribution of 45
meaninglessness 85, 88, 105
megalomania 85, 93, 95, 105
memory 39, 44, 127
    and desire 3, 99ff, 112
Mendelleyeff, periodic table of
    39, 57
mental pain 49, 67, 68, 88, 93,
    98, 103, 114, 119
    see also anxiety
mind/mental apparatus, models
    49, 63
    aesthetic 81, 93, 92, 103, 134
    astronomical 65, 80
    chemical/valency 8, 14, 56,
        57, 58, 60, 72

diamond cutter 134
digestive analogy 35, 38, 44
Grid *see* Grid
lake (transformation) 78
mathematical 84, 88, 91–97,
    99
vs. proto-mental 41
religious vertex 100
    see also growth, mental;
        learning from experience;
        lies; proto-mental func
        tioning
mindlessness 125
models of the mind *see* mind
Money-Kyrle, R. E. 12, 61
morality 66, 81
    and lies 119
    vs. science 36
    sexual 102
myth/mythology 58, 61, 103, 124
    of alpha-function 44, 49, 50,
        52
    apparatus 39–40
    Babel 15
    fixing of 67, 69
    in Grid 66–68, 72, 81, 83,
        113
    Oedipus 13, 32, 66
    Tree of Knowledge 66
nameless dread *see* anxiety
narcissism 7, 10, 13, 120, 123
    limitations of theory 27
negative capability (Keats) 104,
    113, 115
Newton, I. 95
no-thing(s) 86
    mathematical representation
        88
    see also object, as no-thing
O (ultimate reality) 110
    and catastrophic change 93
    inaccessibility of 94

and K-link 49, 84, 92, 94
thought and thinker 118
transformations in 78, 93,
    104
of treatment situation 80, 95
    see also knowledge, search
    for; truth
object(s), internal
    absent 52, 84–88, 92
    attacked/mutilated 129, 130
    bad 48, 122
    bizarre 24, 33, 50, 88, 98,
        128
    combined 9, 27
    containing meaning 71, 84,
        98
    dead 119
    envy of 115
    external 22, 121
    Klein's view 71, 103, 105, 112
    and learning from experience
    as no-thing 86
    part-object 13, 14, 31, 38, 43,
        45, 77, 122
    religious plane 94
    and self 43, 62, 71, 98, 121,
        122, 129
    splitting 23, 34, 121
    'super'-ego 53
        see also bizarre object;
            breast; psychoanalytical
            objects
observation, psychoanalytical 77,
    80, 88, 103, 106, 112
    vs. action 51
    Bion's power of 27, 28, 61
    vs. memory 106
    notation for 91-92
    widening of 9, 20, 21
obsessional phenomena 123, 125
Oedipus/oedipal states 9, 16, 38,
    122

myth of 13, 32, 66, 72
omnipotence/omniscience 35, 38,
    121, 122, 123
    Klein's view 22, 51, 129
paranoid-schizoid position 10, 14,
    33, 65, 71, 106, 124
    and depressive position, oscil-
        lation Ps↔D 56, 61, 65, 71
    and Klein's view 21, 25, 35,
        61, 87, 115, 119
    in psychosis
    and minus K 49, 53, 84, 87,
        93
passion
    as LHK 58, 66, 83
    as psychoanalytic object
        (Grid) 69, 72, 78, 83, 91
        see also emotions, conflict
personality/self
    capable of maturation 94,
        115, 122
    'fiend' part 106, 114, 125
    and K/ truth 50, 53
    Money-Kyrle's view 61
    non-unified 5, 17, 23, 24–25,
        27, 52, 81, 89, 93, 94, 103
    psychotic part 33, 34, 49, 79
    reflected 123
        see also object(s), self
Plato 34, 78, 85, 93, 124
pleasure and reality principles 23,
    389, 43, 102, 107, 121
Poincaré, H. 60, 61
pre-conception
    of breast 52
    conception as 94, 98
    in Grid 57, 60, 81
    and dream/myth 66, 68
    and negative realization 35
    and realization 34, 62, 67, 71,
        103
    unobservable 87

primal scene
  and conjunction of objects 27
  and pairing basic assumption
    9, 14
projective identification
  into analyst 13, 68
  as communication 52, 124
  and container-contained 56
  excessive 33, 34, 38, 48
  and introjective 121
  reversed 24
  and 'super'-ego 81
  'transformation' 77
proto-mental functioning 7, 8,
    10, 13, 18, 41
psychic reality *see* inner world
psychoanalysis
  as game 55, 66, 77, 91, 96
  as messianic idea 110
  method of 3, 9, 20, 21, 37,
    47, 51, 80, 106, 115, 120,
    134
  patience and security in
    114–115
  technique, with psychosis
  as thing-in-itself
    see also interpretation;
      mind; transference
psychoanalyst
  opinion of 81, 84, 92, 98,
    125
  personality of 80, 83, 101
    see also countertransference
psychoanalytical objects 56–64,
    69, 73, 78, 81, 83
psychosis 20, 28, 37, 49, 52, 68,
    106, 107
  and neurosis (Freud) 27
  psychotic part 29, 33, 34, 79
  and schizophrenia 25
Racker, H. 12
reality

vs. delusion 114, 125
external and internal 26, 51,
  58, 62, 67, 102, 120
hatred/denial of 25, 26, 33,
  50, 82, 122, 123
principle 23, 35, 43, 79, 106,
  121
psychic 71, 84, 86, 88, 104,
  107, 113
ultimate (O) 93, 94, 110
testing 17, 50, 81, 85, 98
and work group 9
see also inner world
Reichmann, F. F. 19
religious vertex 110, 111
reverie *see* maternal reverie
reversible perspective 3, 67, 70, 87
Rickman, J. 11
Rosen, J. 19
schizoid mechanisms 21, 22, 122,
  123
  Klein's paper 12, 19, 39
schizophrenia 19ff, 91, 97, 127
  fixation point for 21, 25
  world destruction phantasy
    22
scientific deductive system (Grid)
  57, 58, 61, 66, 69, 103, 123
  and passion 72
Sechehaye, Mme 19
selected fact 3, 61, 63, 65, 72,
  110, 124
self *see* personality; object(s), and
  self
Segal, Hanna 20, 22, 62
sense organs 28
  consciousness as 34
spaces, mental *see* internal world
splitting processes 12, 12, 16, 17,
  22–26, 30, 39, 52, 77, 89,
  121, 123, 129
  and idealization 10, 14, 19,

33, 94
and reintegration 33, 61, 103, 122
Strachey, J. 15
superego
in structural model (Freud) 102, 120
'super'-ego (Bion) 53, 79, 81, 114
symbol formation 15, 17, 21, 27, 118, 124
 vs. notational system 62
 vs. signs 46–48, 62, 77
 see also alpha-function
symbiotic relationship see container–contained
thing-in-itself 50, 63, 97, 105
Kantian 93
psychoanalysis as 111
thought/thinking
and action 15, 20, 59, 67, 97, 102, 113, 115
and anti-thought 92, 125
apparatus for 35, 60
Freud's view 51, 78, 118, 120
genesis of 57
growth of (Grid) 66–70, 98, 123, 124, 125
theory of 27, 29ff, 38
and thinker 118
verbal 22, 23, 24, 25, 30, 31, 32, 33, 111
 see also container–contained; meaning; pre-conception
transference 13, 69, 72, 98, 103, 106, 120, 122
 vs. early memories 20, 30, 77, 95
and group phenomena 8–9
 see also countertransference

truth
absolute (O) 119
and aesthetic intuition 82, 92, 103
explosiveness 96
and K-link 84
 vs. lies 119
nourishment by 36, 38, 49, 50, 56, 79, 107, 113, 124
passively known 114, 117, 118
sense of 35, 51
toleration of uncertainty 94, 98
 see also knowledge, search for; O
uncertainty 63, 65, 67, 94, 113, 121
as negative capability (Keats) 115
values, in Kleinian theory 35, 42, 62, 65, 72, 80, 85, 88, 92, 98, 103, 122
in Bion 113, 124
in 'transformations' 79
vertices, concept of 3, 87, 94, 110
and binocular vision 51, 88, 92
as points of view 82, 84
and positions 87
and reality testing 85
sensuous 84
Wexler, M. 19
Winnicott, D. W. 12
Wittgenstein, L. 21, 49, 85
work group 8, 9, 14, 15
and basic assumption group 14
parents as 9
and psychoanalytic couple 9